ALL
Orig

CAUTION: Professionals and amateurs are hereby warned that this play is subject to royalty. It is fully protected by Original Works Publishing, and the copyright laws of the United States. All rights, including professional, amateur, motion pictures, recitation, lecturing, public reading, radio broadcasting, television, and the rights of translation into foreign languages are strictly reserved.

The performance rights to this play are controlled by Original Works Publishing and royalty arrangements and licenses must be secured well in advance of presentation. PLEASE NOTE that amateur royalty fees are set upon application in accordance with your producing circumstances. When applying for a royalty quotation and license please give us the number of performances intended, dates of production, your seating capacity and admission fee. Royalties are payable with negotiation from Original Works Publishing.

Royalty of the required amount must be paid whether the play is presented for charity or gain and whether or not admission is charged. Particular emphasis is laid on the question of amateur or professional readings, permission and terms for which must be secured from Original Works Publishing through direct contact.

Copying from this book in whole or in part is strictly forbidden by law, and the right of performance is not transferable.

Whenever the play is produced the following notice must appear on all programs, printing, and advertising for the play:

"Produced by special arrangement with
Original Works Publishing.
www.originalworksonline.com"

Due authorship credit must be given on all programs, printing and advertising for the play.

*The Mighty Scarabs*
© Cornell Hubert Calhoun III
Trade Edition, 2016
ISBN 978-1-63092-087-6

*Also Available From
Original Works Publishing*

**Harry and the Thief** by Sigrid Gilmer

**Synopsis:** Mimi's cousin Jeremy has a PhD in physics, a brand new time machine and a plan. He's sending Mimi, a professional thief, back to 1863 to change history by providing Harriet Tubman with modern day guns. Lots and lots of guns.

**Cast Size:** Diverse Cast of 10 Actors

*"Audacious, hysterically funny, irreverent and joyful."*
—Suzan-Lori Parks

# THE MIGHTY SCARABS!
## (An East Tech Story)

## A Play in Two Acts

## by Cornell Hubert Calhoun III

*for June Bailey*

***THE MIGHTY SCARABS*** received its World Premiere on March 6, 2015 at the Karamu Theater in Cleveland, Ohio. It was directed by Christopher Johnston; the scene & lighting design was by Richard M. Morris; the costume design was by Harold Crawford and the stage manager was Gerri Harris. The cast was as follows:

JUNE BAILEY - Prophet D. Seay

RICKS - Titus Covington

SIX-FIVE - Michael Head

GABBY - Caris Collins

JAMAICA PEARL - Lauren Nicole Sturdivant

GIRLENA - Katrice Monee Headd

JOHNNY DOLLAR - Rodney Freeman

JIMMY LOVE - Tyrelle Hariston

KILLER - Reginald McAlpine

# Characters

**1. June Bailey:** Resident, Former East Tech basketball star, early thirties, a self-made poet, Gabby's mentor.

**2. Six-Five:** Very tall, handsome, early thirties, ex-East Tech basketball player, now drives the big rigs.

**3. Girlena Chatman:** Resident, early thirties, attractive, a former East Tech cheerleader, defined by her gorgeous legs, works at a local bar, has a history of choosing the wrong men.

**4. Ricks:** Ex-basketball star, early thirties, mailman, played with June Bailey, Six-Five, and Jimmy Love on the team that was the first all-black high school to win the state championship, has always loved Girlena.

**5. Johnny Dollar:** Numbers man, middle 60s, flashy, colorful, and funny. Takes pride in being the community's numbers runner.

**6. Gabby Chatman:** Resident, 11, Girlena's daughter, bright, articulate, glowing, a new poet.

**7. Jimmy Love:** Member of the East Tech basketball team, early thirties, a man long addicted to drugs.

**8. Charles "Killer" Davis:** Ex-con, former boyfriend of Girlena, a real killer, incarcerated for twelve years, and on his way home to East 55th Street.

**9. Jamaica Pearl:** A most gorgeous streetwalker, former student at East Tech, haunted by her mother's demons, "property" of King Willie II.

**Time:** First day of summer, June 1968. 9 p.m.

**Place:** Cleveland, Ohio.

**Setting:** The scene is the rear of an old four-suite brick apartment building located at **2158 *East 55th***. The building extends from **Left** to **Right**. The rear entrance to the building is located **Up Center**. A small wooden porch with two steps extends from the entrance. There are four windows, two upstairs and two downstairs at the rear of the building. Next to the entrance **Right** mailboxes are placed on the back wall. A large security light glows from the side on the building near the entrance. **Down Right** is an old rusted metal basketball hoop with a tattered net. An old leather basketball lies near the hoop. A trash can is located **Down Left**. A small card table is placed **Center**. Four white weather-beaten lawn chairs are placed around the table. On the table is a radio playing the Temptations hit, *"The Girl's Alright with Me."*

# THE MIGHTY SCARABS

## Prologue

*(Light comes up on an old basketball hoop in the rear of a red brick apartment building located in the heart of the inner city.)*

**Radio Broadcast:** *Booma-lacka*
*Booma-lacka*
*Rah! Rah! Rah!*
*Chicka-lacka*
*Chicka-lacka*
*Cha! Cha! Cha!*
*Booma-lacka*
*Chicka-lacka*
*Rub a dub dub*

*We've got LaSalle over the tub,*
*We gonna wash 'em out,*
*Ring 'em out,*
*Hang 'em on the line!*
*We'll beat LaSalle any ole time!*
*Any ole time!*
*Any ole time!*

**Announcer:** We're in St John's Arena on the campus of Ohio State University. The Ohio High School Basketball Division II State Basketball Championship. Cleveland East Tech trailing Cincinnati LaSalle 57-56! Eighteen Seconds left on the clock. This is East Tech's last chance. Right here. Right now. June Bailey to inbound. Quick pass to Ricks on the right wing. Ricks dribbles left, inside to Junior Payne, back out to Jimmy Love, across to Fast Eddie Cain at the top of the key. Fast Eddie Cain passes to June Bailey, June

Bailey dribbles left, spins, gets by his defender in the lane, ball in the air. Everyone on their feet...

*(Static as lights fade to black.)*

# ACT I

***"Sometimes you eat the bear.
Sometimes the bear eats you..."***

## SCENE I

**Time:**  First day of summer, June 1968
9 p.m.

**Place:**  Cleveland, Ohio.

**At Rise:**

*(Jamaica Pearl enters from Right. She is a very attractive woman in her twenties. Her skirt is very, very short. Her body is wonderfully sculpted. She gazes at the apartment building, places some money in her garter, and exits.*

*Girlena Chatman enters from Left. She is a woman in her early thirties. She wears a stunning black dress that shows off her figure and gorgeous pair of curvaceous bow legs that have always been her signature. She crosses to table, sits, and starts to silently look through an obituary. The Temptations' hit fades out, and a lively local DJ can be heard.)*

**Radio**:
> Bitty-Bop, Bitty-Bop, Bip Bop Bam,
> You with Uncle Paul on an all day jam,
> Now you can change your radio station, baby
> that ain't no crime,
> but Uncle Paul plays all the hits,
> all the time.

It's the first day of summer, 1968. Jus' a lovely evenin' in the inner city, twilight stretching along from the bricks of the stoic East Tech High School building to the projects at Carver Park. Now all y'all know things go better with Coke. So put the brown bags down and run on over to Troy's Ford Mart at the corner of East 43rd and Cedar, and get yourself a cold one to go. *(Drinking)* Ah. Troy's... where the conversations range from Politics to Lovemaking, from Numbers to Prostitution... from Civil Rights to Human Rights. Troy is the Man, the Mentor, the Arbitrator, the Regulator. Well, there's a full moon in the month of June, and Uncle Paul gonna thrill y'all with this next tune. We got more of the Temptin' Temptations, y'all. They be in town later this summer, appearing live at Leo's Casino. Stayed tuned for details. This is y'all Uncle Paul, radio station, 890 AM, WKMU Cleveland, Ohio. The sooooooooooul of the city, baby.

*(June Bailey enters from 2158. He is a handsome man in his early thirties. He walks with a cane, and wears a once stylish straw hat. He crosses to table and turns radio down. He stares at the basketball hoop with reservation.)*

**JUNE BAILEY:** Damn!

**GIRLENA:** *(Pause)* What's eating at you tonight, June Bailey?

**JUNE BAILEY:** I jus' wish I was somewheres else sometimes; that's all.

**GIRLENA:** Where else any of us gonna be but on East 55th Street?

**JUNE BAILEY:** Yeah, I know. *(Pause)* How was it?

**GIRLENA:** Wills put him away nice. Yellow suit. Yellow straw hat. Yellow casket. Funeral's tomorrow at 10 o'clock.

**JUNE BAILEY:** Old Man Wills didn't figure out a way to stretch him out in that yellow GTO?

**GIRLENA:** The GTO was parked in front of the funeral home. Two women had the nerve to get in it. Wills made 'em get out. Wills pulled it around back after that.

**JUNE BAILEY:** Pontiac GTO. Mellow yellow. Only thing I don't like is those birth control seats. Hear what I say?

**GIRLENA:** Birth control seats?

**JUNE BAILEY:** Bucket seats.

**GIRLENA:** That would cramp your style, wouldn't it, June Bailey?

**JUNE BAILEY:** Ain't nobody got time for no bucket seats. Birth control seats. Bench seats put your gal right next to you. All you have to do is reach out and touch --

**GIRLENA**: Please.

**JUNE BAILEY:** *(Laughing)* Slipping and sliding all night loooooong. Hear what I say?

**GIRLENA:** Bucket seats will do me just fine, June Bailey. I don't like sitting on top of a man. Hear what I say?

**JUNE BAILEY:** I hear you. *(Pause)* Johnny Dollar said they spent close to ten thousand dollars on the funeral.

**GIRLENA:** Please.

**JUNE BAILEY:** Said there were at least one hundred flower arrangements around the casket.

**GIRLENA:** I didn't see that.

**JUNE BAILEY:** Some of the flower arrangements read - --- **We Remember '55.**

**GIRLENA:** I saw that!

**JUNE BAILEY:** Johnny Dollar said they buried him with hundred dollar bills in each hand, diamonds on every finger, and ten gold chains around his neck. Said they put diamonds and jewels right in the casket with him. Said Old Man Wills had to hire security guards to stand by the casket. Had the Cleveland Police parked in front of the funeral home.

**GIRLENA:** Please.

**JUNE BAILEY:** Johnny Dollar said chicks were jus' pushin' and shovin' tryin' to get their last look at him. Old Man Wills had to rope the casket off. **ROPE IT OFF!** Said some chicks started slow dancin' around the casket. Said two chicks started fightin', and went to their baby strollers to get their switchblades.

**GIRLENA:** You know Johnny Dollar ain't never told the truth about nothing. Can't tell the truth about nothing. Couldn't tell the truth if his life depended on it.

**JUNE BAILEY:** Johnny Dollar said the Allen twins walked out of the nursing home all the way up 55th to pay their respects.

**GIRLENA:** June Bailey, please.

**JUNE BAILEY:** Said they wore yellow corduroy jumpsuits in his honor.

**GIRLENA:** Corduroy in June?

**JUNE BAILEY:** Johnny Dollar said the Little Twin was busy stuffing her purse with House of Wills stationery and pens while the Big Twin was taking all the toilet paper and ash trays out of the restroom.

**GIRLENA:** The Allen twins were not at the wake, June Bailey. Besides, Johnny Dollar was too busy writing numbers to see what was going on.

**JUNE BAILEY:** Yep. Johnny Dollar be writin' some numbers. Be writing numbers in Giant Tiger, Kresgee's, Western Auto, Sears & Roebuck, Troy's, even in church. He be yellin' during Bible study, "You want that 721 boxed, straight, or split? You want that 825 in the new stock, old stock, bond, or big bond? Man, I told you that 925 is cut today. The Massario Brothers cut that number five ways."

**GIRLENA:** Reverend Haughton put him out of church last Sunday for writing numbers during Sunday school. He supposed to be reciting from the Bible. He reciting from the dream book. Yelling out God was 749 and the Devil was 822. After Reverend asked him to leave he went out and sat on the church steps and kept writing numbers.

**JUNE BAILEY:** Until the ladies auxiliary was ready with the Sunday Worship Meal of fried chicken, baked chicken---

**JUNE BAILEY/GIRLENA:** Stewed chicken, grilled chicken, broiled chicken, barbecued chicken.

**JUNE BAILEY:** Collard greens, potato salad, creamed corn, candied yams, fried okra, chitterlings, and ---

**JUNE BAILEY/GIRLENA:** Butter baked skillet bread!

**GIRLENA:** Johnny Dollar was first in line. Reverend Haughton just shook his head and walked away.

**JUNE BAILEY:** What was the number today? If that 247 fell, June Bailey gonna get him a new straw hat from Mike the Hatter. Hear what I say?

**GIRLENA:** You better walk down to Troy's, get the evening edition of the Cleveland Press and see if you hit. Miss Girlena Chatman will be glad to help spend your money.

**JUNE BAILEY:** Troy's too crowded now. You know everybody and they momma in there telling Troy their tales of woe.

**GIRLENA:** Folks trust Troy. They respect him.

**JUNE BAILEY:** You got a problem go see Troy.

**GIRLENA:** He solve 'em, don't he?

**JUNE BAILEY:** Every time. Whenever there's a situation in the black community, the Mayor call Troy first.

**GIRLENA:** The Mayor ain't no fool.

**JUNE BAILEY:** When I was a little boy my momma used to send me to Troy's Grocery Mart with her grocery list. Always had to get a loaf of Millbrook white bread and a quart of Sealtest sweet milk. June Bailey always sneak himself a hand full of mint juleps when Troy wasn't looking. Hear what I say?

**GIRLENA:** Don't think Troy didn't know that, June Bailey. You can't slip nothing past Troy Lee James.

**JUNE BAILEY:** *(Laughing)* Troy was saying last week he looking to collect for all them mint juleps I snatched before he retire. I gave him a good number to play. 247!

**GIRLENA:** How you miss the number on the five o'clock news?

**JUNE BAILEY:** Overslept. It don't matter. June Bailey will know soon enough. Johnny Dollar be walking up East 55th in those two sizes too small Verde snakeskin shoes. June Bailey have his hand in the Massario Brothers' pockets for a change then.

**GIRLENA:** *(Pause)* Well, like I said, it was a very nice service.

**JUNE BAILEY:** Johnny Dollar said when he die his funeral gonna be even bigger. Way Bigger! Said he gonna have Boyd & Sons stretch him out.

**GIRLENA:** Boyd's can't do funeral like The House of Wills. Wills know how to put on a wake and funeral.

**JUNE BAILEY:** I feel kinda bad I don't do funerals. Can't remember the last time I was inside a funeral home. Maybe after Diddy shot my daddy in the head. I was ten... maybe eleven. I stayed at Rick's place for two weeks.

**GIRLENA:** You do what's best for you. People deal with death in their own way.

**JUNE BAILEY:** They can throw what's left of June Bailey out in Potter's Field when he die. Hear what I say?

**GIRLENA:** Please!

**JUNE BAILEY:** When you're dead you're dead. You ain't coming back. You ever hear tell of some fool coming back after he was dead? They can throw what's left of June Bailey out in Potter's Field when he die.

**GIRLENA:** Well, I don't wanna be thrown out in no Potter's Field. That's where they bury poor folks who don't have any money, family, or friends.

**JUNE BAILEY:** Or Nationwide. Hear what I say?

**GIRLENA:** You gotta have insurance. My mother taught me that. I got me and Gabby covered. Every other week Mr. Everett Hatfield from Atlanta Life Insurance Company come by 2158. I hand him nine dollars and thirty-eight cents. They'll never throw what's left of Girlena Denise Chatman out in Potter's Field.

**JUNE BAILEY:** Highland, Evergreen, Riverside, Lakeview... Potter's Field. High ground or low ground. It's all dirt. You jus' covered up with dirt.

**GIRLENA:** Well I don't wanna be buried in the ground. I don't want to be on the menu for any worms. I want to be cremated like my grandmother, Miss Nellie Freeman, and the rest of my relatives. Besides, I don't want anyone to make a big fuss.

**JUNE BAILEY:** Jus' turn on the furnace.

**GIRLENA:** Yep.

**JUNE BAILEY:** AND FEEL THE FIRE!

**GIRLENA:** Yep. Almost our entire family's been cremated. After my cousins started shooting at my Aunt Nora's funeral years ago, my mother said never again. My mother was in charge of the arrangements. My cousins took out pistols during the wake and started shooting. Trying to kill each other. Up there at Watson's on 105th. Fighting over a little piece of money my Aunt Nora left everyone. Fools fighting over Fifty-Six dollars and thirty-nine cents that had to be split fourteen different ways.

**JUNE BAILEY:** *(Rising)* Well, if you go before me, I'm gonna send you off real nice, Girlena Chatman. We gonna bronze those pretty bow legs of yours. Put a sign on 'em, "Perfection." Donate 'em to the Health and Loveliness Museum. June Bailey gonna stand up in Reverend Haughton's Cleveland Church of Christ and recite some fine poetry.
*Here lies Girlena Chatman,*
*Lord, ain't she fine,*
*with bow legs divine,*
*I know it was good and plenty,*
*but she very seldom gave up any .....*

Hear what I say?

**GIRLENA:** You crazy, June Bailey.

**JUNE BAILEY:** Wait! Wait!

> *Now I lay me down to slumber,*
> *I pray the Lord I hit the number,*
> *If I die before eleven,*
> *Put fifty cents on 247*

Number gonna be so hot the Massario Brothers liable to cut it... Hear what I say?

**GIRLENA:** You dreaming.

**JUNE BAILEY:** Who ain't still dreaming about... Girlena Denise Chatman?

**GIRLENA:** *(Pause)* Eddie Cain ain't dreaming no more.

**JUNE BAILEY:** Said he still loved you.

**GIRLENA**: Eddie Cain said a lot of crazy things.

**JUNE BAILEY:** Said he was gonna live forever.

**GIRLENA:** He was wrong, wasn't he?

**JUNE BAILEY:** Yep. Guess he was. *(Pause)* Everybody turned out, huh?

**GIRLENA:** Black folks and white folks lined up from the House of Wills all the way down East 55th street. Some had to stand across the street in East Tech's parking lot.

**JUNE BAILEY:** Everyone knew Fast Eddie Cain. Everyone remembers '55.

**GIRLENA:** *(Crossing to porch and sitting)* Some folks were yelling "**55.**" Women were everywhere all down on the floor just yelling and screaming.

**JUNE BAILEY:** I'm sorry but you know a skirt was a skirt to Fast Eddie Cain. Even way back in R. B. Hayes Elementary School. Fast Eddie Cain always had some girl in the cloakroom.

**GIRLENA:** You had your share, too, June Bailey.

**JUNE BAILEY:** Never had you.

**GIRLENA:** I was smart. I got to school early.

**JUNE BAILEY:** Every morning June Bailey and Fast Eddie Cain be hidin' inside the cloakroom. Some of the girls be late, late on purpose. All them girls were crazy about some June Bailey and some Fast Eddie Cain. Hear what I say?

**GIRLENA:** Please.

**JUNE BAILEY:** Y'all come to school wearin' those little plaid skirts with them white bobby socks. Pretty little legs all shined up with that Royal Crown Hair dressing. We'd wait 'til after they put their coats on one of the racks, then we'd grab 'em and press 'em up against the wall... wait 'til they close they eyes and we press our bodies up against 'em... waiting for that first moan ... Then we'd run out... into the hallway... runnin'... That was what you call Cloakroom Heaven.

**GIRLENA:** That was what you call nasty, June Bailey.

**JUNE BAILEY:** We wasn't nasty! We was jus' being boys. Them gals could never get away from me and Fast Eddie Cain. *(Pause)* June Bailey seen you ridin' in that yellow GTO ---

**GIRLENA:** You been spying on me, June Bailey? Gabby said she saw a man in the shadows watching us when we were walking to the Park Theater on 105th two weeks ago. I turned around and didn't see anyone. Was that you?

**JUNE BAILEY:** June Bailey walk every night, Girlena. But June Bailey ain't walking that damn far. East 55th to 105th? This old leg ain't been right since June Bailey fell in that hole at J& L Steel. Doctor said to exercise this leg unless I wanna lose it, so June Bailey exercise this leg.

**GIRLENA:** If it wasn't you, who was it?

**JUNE BAILEY:** Any man in his right mind.

**GIRLENA:** Then you're right. It couldn't have been you.

**JUNE BAILEY:** Too much history between you and Fast Eddie Cain. It ain't over 'til it's over. Hear what I say?

**GIRLENA:** Well it's over now.

*(Ricks enters. He is a man in his early thirties. He is dressed in his postal uniform and carries a bag of mail. He crosses Center to table.)*

**RICKS:** What's up, June Bailey?

**JUNE BAILEY:** Still kicking but not high.

**RICKS:** Greetings, Girlena.

**GIRLENA:** Hey, Ricks. How's it going?

**RICKS:** Just left Ressie Chambers' house. She all broke up over her son Pretty Boy getting drafted into the army. Scared they gonna send him to Viet Nam. He got to report to that Federal Building downtown on Tuesday.

**JUNE BAILEY:** Viet Nam ain't no joke. Harvey Miller just died over there, you know. You remember Harvey Miller? Used to fall asleep all the time in Mr. Whitman's Mechanical Drawing class – Room 345 Harvey always wake up before the bell ring. He take a sheet of that real thin paper, take your drawing and trace it for his. Said Mr. Whitman wouldn't know the difference. Mr. Whitman let him go the entire year. Mr. Whitman ain't say nothing. For the final exam we had to draw this horizontal box thing. Harvey grab London Burnett's drawing just before the bell ring. He trace it up real nice. Hand it to Mr. Whitman. Harvey just grinning. Mr. Whitman say, "What you got there, Harvey?" Harvey say, "This one of my best drawings, Mr. Whit." Mr. Whitman looked at Harvey's drawing and say, "Harvey, this ain't shit. You got an F coming." *(Laughing)* Harvey Miller. They shipped his body down to Alabama. His momma moved down there last year. They didn't have a service up here. Old Man Wills thought he was gonna gets some business when Harvey got killed over there in Nam. He was wrong. I hope Pretty Boy don't have to go.

**GIRLENA:** I'm just glad the army don't draft females. I don't know what I'd do if I got a letter from Uncle Sam saying Gabby had to report when she turned eighteen.

**RICKS:** They drafted Honey Lewis's oldest boy Leroy last year but he didn't have to go. He didn't pass the written test.

**JUNE BAILEY:** Pretty Boy should have answered the questions wrong on purpose. That's what Leroy Lewis done.

**GIRLENA:** I remember when Pretty Boy was running up and down East 55th delivering the Cleveland Press. Time sure flies; that's for sure. *(Rising)* I'll call Troy, June Bailey. See what the number was. *(Slapping him on the behind)* See if I get a chance to spend some of your money.

*(Girlena exits.)*

**RICKS:** *(Sitting)* Man, she still pulls at a man's heart-strings.

**JUNE BAILEY:** Yep. *(Crossing to table)* You know she and Fast Eddie ---

**RICKS:** Hooked up again? I figured as much.

**JUNE BAILEY:** *(Sitting)* Fast Eddie Cain was hangin' around 2158 all the time before ---

**RICKS:** Somebody shot him five times when he was leaving Frenchy's Bar. Had a white girl on each arm. White girls ran.

**JUNE BAILEY:** Gonna be a hard case to solve. Fast Eddie Cain had lots of enemies. Women he hurt, cats he played, and the Massario Brothers, who thought he was getting too big. Hear what I say?

**RICKS:** Girlena always was crazy about some Eddie Cain.

**JUNE BAILEY:** And you always was crazy about some Girlena Chatman.

**RICKS:** She always was good at teasing my heart. Still does. I admit that.

**JUNE BAILEY:** You should have made your move 'fore Killer made his. When she and Fast Eddie Cain broke up the first time, you should have made your move then.

**RICKS:** What did she ever see in that fool?

**JUNE BAILEY:** Fast Eddie Cain always had a slew of women. She was with Fast Eddie Cain while she was fooling 'round with Killer. When Killer found out she was still messing around with Fast Eddie Cain it drove Killer over the edge. He was already nuts.

**RICKS:** He went nuts after Coach Chavers cut him.

**JUNE BAILEY:** Which time? He got cut every year.

**RICKS:** Couldn't make a lay-up.

**JUNE BAILEY:** Couldn't hold on to the damn ball.

**RICKS:** Couldn't make Junior Varsity in the 12$^{th}$ grade, even if they would have let 12$^{th}$ graders play JV.

**JUNE:** He was terrible. *(Pause)* He getting out of the joint in a couple of weeks.

**RICKS:** Girlena know?

**JUNE BAILEY:** Yeah, but she been real quiet about it though. Killer been gone... what, twelve, thirteen years?

**RICKS:** Killed Neecee's cousin in front of Ellis Bar. Boy had jus' come up here from Alabama. If Neecee's cousin had been white, Killer would have got the chair.

**JUNE BAILEY:** You know he headin' straight for 2158 East 55th... and Girlena.

**RICKS:** He know 'bout Gabby? He know who Gabby's father is? Talk about a storm coming.

**JUNE BAILEY:** If Fast Eddie Cain was still alive... drop you and Six-Five in the mix.

**RICKS:** I ain't never hid my feelings for Girlena, June Bailey.

**JUNE BAILEY:** Charles "Killer" Davis ain't forgot that either. Y'all was some real hoodlums back then.

**RICKS:** You wasn't no saint, June Bailey. I remember when you carried two pistols. You lied, you stole, you cheated, and you shot folks.

**JUNE BAILEY:** I know my past. God knows what I done. I ain't doin' it now, but I could do it again. You better keep your pistol handy, Ricks. Hear what I say?

**RICKS:** I'm gonna always do that. Keep my shotgun handy, too.

**JUNE BAILEY:** You do that. You might need it. Foolin' 'round down here on East 55th ain't no joke.

**RICKS:** I hear ya. I hope you know where your pistol is?

**JUNE BAILEY:** Might be in my pocket.

**RICKS**: Mine is.

**JUNE BAILEY:** I hear ya, Ricks.

**RICKS:** I'm glad you do. *(Rising)* I still can't figure Girlena out.

**JUNE BAILEY:** Man, if a chick ain't with you in your mix, she with someone else in theirs. You gotta let a chick choose. If they don't choose you, smile and walk away. Wait until you get chose. Hear what I say? When a chick choose you, when you chosen, you set then. Been livin' by that theory since elementary school when I first looked at Girlena Chatman and she looked at Eddie Cain. I jus' smiled and walked away. I waited to get chose.

**RICKS:** We all got chose in high school. Yeah, remember the parties at Ms. Brister's house after the games? You come in cold and leave out WARM.

**JUNE BAILEY:** Man, East Tech had some fine chicks, man. Pat Riley, Ressie Chambers, Norma Fluker, Donella Reese, Carmen Sledge, Jessie Larkins. Man, remember Jessie Larkins?

**RICKS:** Too, too fine. We was ball players. We played for East Tech. We kept all the chicks smiling, didn't we? All but Girlena.

**JUNE BAILEY:** Girlena wasn't playin'.

**RICKS:** Well, Eddie Cain played her.

**JUNE BAILEY:** They played each other... over and over... but Fast Eddie Cain ain't playing no more. Fast Eddie Cain played his last game. Hear what I say?

*(Lights fade to black as "Since I lost My Baby" plays.)*

# SCENE II

**Time:** Friday afternoon. The following day.

**At Rise:**

*("Since I Lost My Baby" by The Temptations blares from radio. Girlena Chapman sits at the table wearing a pretty yellow dress. She sings as she looks through an old high school yearbook.)*

**GIRLENA:** *(Singing)*
Since I lost my baby.
Oh, since I lost my baby.

*(Jimmy Love enters. He is a slender man in his early thirties, but looks much older due to his life style. He is dressed in an old dirty t-shirt, jeans, sneakers, and old baseball cap.)*

**LOVE:** Hey, Girlena. *(Searching)* June Bailey around?

**GIRLENA:** You see him? *(Pause)* Naw, he ain't.

**LOVE:** I just come by to say… say I'm sorry.

**GIRLENA:** Didn't see you at the wake or funeral.

**LOVE:** Yeah. Yeah. I was ah… ah sort of tied up. I had some things… some stuff goin' on.

**GIRLENA:** Please.

**LOVE:** But Fast Eddie Cain was a true teammate 'til the end.

**GIRLENA:** Helped keep you in your goods, huh?

**LOVE:** What?

**GIRLENA:** You need to clean yourself up once and for all, Jimmy Love. Fast Eddie Cain ain't gonna be around to keep you in your stuff no more.

**LOVE:** Yeah. Yeah. I been thinking about that, been thinking on it long and strong. *(Pause)* Don't know when June Bailey's coming back, huh?

**GIRLENA:** You know I'm right.

**LOVE:** I'm gonna work on taming that bear right away, Girlena. Go on down to the Charity and check myself in, maybe in a week or so. Big Edgar went down last week. Said they got nice soft pillows, clean bed sheets, and good grub. Said they treated him like a basketball star.

**GIRLENA:** If Big Edgar was doin' any rehab he got a twin down there at Charity. Big Edgar was in Ellis Bar last night looking to score. Looking to buy some heroin from Mr. Walter.

**LOVE:** Well, he was there one night last week. Said no one on East 55th expected him to clean himself up so he checked himself out.

**GIRLENA:** Please. Go on, Jimmy Love.

**LOVE:** *(Playing with cap)* I been trying hard to get this bear off my back but the big black sucker won't budge. He a real feisty one.

**GIRLENA:** That bear sure ain't gonna budge if you ain't fighting to get him off you.

**LOVE:** He been riding me for a long time. Right when I think I got the best of him, he sends for that sweet white boy who washes all my sins away...

**GIRLENA:** I don't wanna hear it, Jimmy Love! You do dope because you want to do dope, because you don't want to face reality. You do dope to escape responsibility. When a junkie needs junk he'll do anything to get it. You name it, a junkie will do it. Steal, rob or even put a knife in his own brother's back.

**LOVE:** Yeah. Yeah. I know. Anything and everything that goes wrong in this world gets blamed on dope. Some wild eyed young boy rapes his schoolteacher and he's full of dope. A group of corner boys full of goofballs or stoned on cough syrup do anything, they high on junk. Society don't have a clue. They don't know where it's at. A junkie on dope don't bother nobody. He too busy living the slow-down life, the mellow life, MY life. I ain't blaming nobody for what I am. People need to understand something before they start condemning it, putting it down. It's just another case of ignorance before investigation. It's like they say, you can take the dope from the junkie, but you can't take the junkie from the dope.

**GIRLENA:** You should want a better life for yourself, Jimmy Love. How that gonna happen when you full of junk?

**LOVE:** Jimmy Love ain't bothering nobody. Jimmy Love ain't doing nothing. I ain't drafting no folks to fight in the army over there in Nam. I ain't killing up no folks. I ain't built no bombs or flown no planes dropping none. Why folks wanna mess with me? All I'm looking for is a little peace, a little happiness. All

I'm doing is looking for the High Life. Folks wanna bring me down and call me all out my name, saying my kind is the worst kind in the world while they killing folks in other countries by the thousands. I ain't done nothing to nobody. I ain't shot nobody. All I do is shoot dope. All I do is let that bad boy floats my cares away down a sweet river of "I don't even care no more." It sure beats what all these hypocrites is doing.

**GIRLENA:** So that's your excuse for giving up, for shooting up, for not being able to change the world? *(Pause)* Please. That's pitiful if you ask me, Jimmy Love.

**LOVE:** Well, ain't nobody asked you, Girlena. I'm a dope fiend. I do dope and I love it.

**GIRLENA:** That same dope is gonna kill you one day, Jimmy Love.

**LOVE:** Lotta things on East 55th can kill you, Girlena. You just wait 'til it happen. You just wait your turn.

*(They stare at each other.)*

**GIRLENA:** *(Pause)* June Bailey may be down at Troy's.

**LOVE:** Huh? Naw. He ain't at Troy's. *(Pause)* I just come from Troy's. Some white fellow in there say he a civil rights worker. He trying to get folks to protest against Sealtest. Say Sealtest got all them employees and ain't none of 'em black. But say Sealtest got all they white milk in all black neighborhood stores. Hunchy told the white fellow, name Mr. Henry Roy. Hunchy say, "Ain't nobody on East 55th thinking about protesting or demonstrating about nothing, 'cept for more wine, more dope, more whores, and maybe a good number." Hunchy told him, say, "it might take another hundred years for folks 'round here to understand what he saying, let alone do something about it. If you ain't got no dollars to give away, you may as well walk away." Fellow didn't get down on himself one bit though. Kept right on preaching 'bout the injustices that Sealtest and other white companies like 'em was doing to black folks. With that he started buying everyone in Troy's rounds of cold sodas. Troy made a killing selling Royal Crown Cola this afternoon.

GIRLENA: That white man should know you can't talk about freedom and civil rights to people down here. Black civil rights workers can't reach 'em, let alone white ones. Folks down here don't wanna hear that, because they don't wanna change. Nobody likes change anyhow.

LOVE: Yeah. Well Mr. Henry Roy say poor black folks 'round here ain't no different than poor black folks everywhere. All they need is an education. Say all that has to happen is for black folks to get educated, get used to trying new and different things. Say all that has to happen is for someone to show 'em the right way. Black Folks will go through life doing things the wrong way unless there's someone to show 'em the right way. They'll continue to do things the wrong way even if it kills 'em, and they know it's killing 'em, unless they shown something better. That's what Mr. Henry Roy say.

GIRLENA: What the people say?

**LOVE:** People ain't said nothing. The people just sat there and drank they cold sodas. Troy ain't said nothing either, Troy just waited for Mr. Henry Roy to pay for all them cold Royal Crown Colas the people was drinking. Mr. Henry Roy paid Troy and left. Said he'd be back though. Said he wasn't near done. Left a paper for folks to sign. Hunchy turned the paper over and started writing out his numbers on it 'bout the same time Johnny Dollar walked in.

**GIRLENA:** I hope this Henry Roy, white civil rights worker stays clear of Ellis Bar. Black folks enjoying they liquor after a hard day of hustlin'don't take kindly to no civil rights workers, black or white. And the hustlers -- they thrive on the downtrodden. They work hard at keeping their people down so they can't always have the advantage.

**LOVE:** All folks 'round here looking for is some good dope, a good woman, or a good number. After Mr. Henry Roy walked out, all the attention turned to across the street where Jamaica Pearl was standing. All the fellows crowded against the window to get a good long look. Twitchy Mitchell say he ain't seen a woman built up like Jamaica Pearl since her momma, Red Delilah. Say Jamaica Pearl belong on the cover of Ebony Magazine. Maybe even Life or Time. Twitchy Mitchell say Jamaica Pearl made her pimp King Willie II so much money last year he bought himself a new pink Fleetwood with silver skirts. Everybody got a real treat when she walked into Troy's to buy herself some Mint Juleps and a pack of Pall Malls. Two or three cats offered to pay for her purchases but she say, "No, thanks fellows. Jamaica Pearl always got her own," in that sweet voice of hers. Jamaica Pearl sure know where it's at, I tell you. She turned 'round and strolled out of Troy's on that fine pair of walking legs... 'course, they not nearly as fine and sturdy as the bow legged pair you walking on, Girlena,

**GIRLENA:** Um Um Um ...

**LOVE:** *(Pause)* I hear Killer getting out soon.

**GIRLENA:** That's what I hear. Guess you better start running, Jimmy Love.

*(Six-Five enters. He is a very tall brown skinned man in his early thirties.)*

**SIX-FIVE:** Hey, Girlena.

**GIRLENA:** Hey, Six-Five.

**LOVE:** The rebounding machine, Junior Payne, better known as Six-Five. Starting Center! East Tech Scarabs! Number thirty-two home white, thirty-three away in gold!

**SIX-FIVE:** What you doing around 2158, Jimmy Love?

**LOVE:** Huh? Ah... I stopped by to offer Girlena my condolences. And now I'm gone. See you, Girlena. Tell June Bailey I stopped by on the real.

*(Love exits.)*

**SIX-FIVE:** How long he been here?

**GIRLENA:** Not long.

**SIX-FIVE:** Only one of us who went to class and made good grades. Could have been anything. Never put any of that education to any good use at all. Number Twenty white, twenty one gold. *(Pause)* I'm sorry. You alright? I was on that two-week west coast run when I heard.

**GIRLENA:** They buried him today.

**SIX-FIVE:** I know. I tried to reach you. Gabby said you were gone. Called June Bailey, but his damn phone just rang. Don't know why he has one. He never answers it. Hell, he never uses it unless he calling in his numbers. *(Pause)* You look lovely as usual. Very pretty dress. Yellow, huh?

**GIRLENA:** Eddie bought it a few weeks ago. You know how Eddie loved him some yellow, loved seeing me in some yellow all the time, even had me wear yellow slips, said some yellow showed off my legs.

**SIX-FIVE:** Any color dress do that.

**GIRLENA:** Please.

**SIX-FIVE:** My rig broke down near Toledo. You know they give a black man the worst truck to drive. Had to wait 'til they repaired it. Tried to reach you. Figured there was nothing I could do. Jus' pulled in about an hour ago.

**GIRLENA:** Gabby told me you called. Thank you. *(Taking a deep breath)* I'm Okay.

**SIX-FIVE:** Where is Ms. Gabby?

**GIRLENA:** Up there at Fairfax, shooting baskets with June Bailey.

**SIX-FIVE:** Gabby can shoot the lights out already. I watched her in Central Playground the other day. I tell Ricks all the time she shoots better than him when we was playing.

**GIRLENA:** Y'all had her shooting baskets since she could hold a ball.

**SIX-FIVE:** She loves it, too. The way we did when we were coming up. Used to clear the snow off the court at Central Playground. We used to play by the streetlight and moonlight after dark. Too bad they don't let girls play. Maybe one day folks will come out and cheer the girls when they play other schools. *(Pause)* Any leads on who killed Fast Eddie Cain?

**GIRLENA:** The Police have questioned almost everyone. Talking to some folks twice. If they got any leads they ain't saying.

**SIX-FIVE:** Ricks been around?

**GIRLENA:** Seen him at the funeral.

**SIX-FIVE:** Why you and Ricks never hooked up? He always been crazy about you?

**GIRLENA:** *(Pause)* Maybe cause he never came to me. A woman don't wanna think, she wanna know.

**SIX-FIVE:** Ricks and June Bailey always thought me and you were---

**GIRLENA:** Lotta nosey folks on 55th did. If a girl stay with a guy it gotta be about lying down. It can't just be about she and her daughter needing a place to stay. I'll always be grateful for that, Six-Five. You was a real friend to me. You was on the road most of the time and made your place available to me and Gabby. Folks gonna believe what they wanna believe.

**SIX-FIVE:** I guess June Bailey figured you and Gabby should have moved in with him.

**GIRLENA:** Well, June Bailey figured wrong. You know it's a lot more drama than meets the eye when it comes to me and June Bailey. Many folks just don't know. I wasn't gonna be sliding down that hill no time soon. Ricks and June Bailey can figure what they wanna.

**SIX-FIVE:** How's Gabby holding up?

**GIRLENA:** She didn't say much when I told her about Eddie. Just took her ball and went out and start shooting baskets. She didn't wanna go to the funeral, and I didn't make her. She's like June Bailey. Not afraid of death, but determined to deal with it on her own terms. She and Eddie shared some emotions... some feelings... They had their moments, good and bad. He wasn't a bad father, just didn't really know how to be a good one. With the life style he led, she didn't see him much. When they did see each other, it was here in this yard, at Central playground, or he'd ride her up to Fairfax. Never talking much ... just shooting baskets... she trying her best to out shoot him... focused... driven... like y'all were... in '55.

**SIX-FIVE:** You think the mob killed Fast Eddie Cain?

**GIRLENA:** The Massario Brothers? *(Pause)* Rumors are they're behind the killings of Scatter and Slim Jim. They ain't never had no love for black folks. I know they were feuding over the boundaries of black and white territories. Everybody wants a piece of the number's game.

**SIX-FIVE:** Number's game is big money. Almost as big as the dope game. The Massario Brothers got they hands in both, just like Fast Eddie Cain. *(Pause)* You gonna ever tell Gabby?

**GIRLENA:** No.

**SIX-FIVE:** You Okay with that, Girlena?

**GIRLENA:** Yep.

**SIX-FIVE:** Even now that ...

**GIRLENA:** I said I would never tell her, Six-Five.

**SIX-FIVE:** What you gonna do about Killer? You know he heading straight to 2158 East 55th when he get out.

**GIRLENA:** Been thinking about going to Chicago... again.

**SIX-FIVE:** Chicago?

**GIRLENA:** Gabby was born there. Remember? I left Cleveland two summers after we graduated... confused... crying... pregnant. Stayed with my Aunt Lilly. I still got family up there. *(Pause)* Me and Gabby gonna be on one of those double-decker Greyhounds to Chicago. Always wanted to ride a double-decker... First time I went to Chicago I was on a small bus.

*(Johnny Dollar enters. He is a tall well-dressed black man in his early sixties. He wears an expensive leisure suit and carries a small notepad. He walks gingerly.)*

**JOHNNY DOLLAR:** Good night, Irene.

**SIX-FIVE:** John Dollar.

**GIRLENA:** Hey, Johnny Dollar?

**JOHNNY DOLLAR:** These snakeskin shoes is talking to my toe jams.

**SIX-FIVE:** Can't wear a eleven if you got size thirteen feet.

**JOHNNY DOLLAR:** Verde snakeskin don't come in thirteen. Eleven the largest size they come. Johnny Dollar had to make do. *(Sitting and taking off shoes)* Whew. Where June Bailey? His 247 is hot. Red Hot. You can get it or not. You can play if you're going my way, or you can miss out, and hit the highway. Be there or be square. If you a lame, Johnny Dollar ain't to blame. I'm on my way to see the Massario Brothers.

**GIRLENA:** June Bailey at Fairfax.

**JOHNNY DOLLAR:** He told me to stop by 2158. He called in some numbers but left 247 off. I don't wanna hear him crying at 5 o'clock if that number come out.

**GIRLENA:** How he forget 247? He been playing that number for a year. Says he keeps dreaming about our old junior high homeroom teacher, Ms. Hamilton. That was her room number, 247.

**JOHNNY DOLLAR:** Maybe he's off his medication. I jus' left Troy's. Hunchy over there crying 'cause he'd been playing 486 all week. Yesterday it came 684. I told that fool to box his numbers. He was crying last week after he hit 529. I told him to put a dollar on the number instead of a dime. Fool could've been back in the race.

**GIRLENA:** I don't know why people waste their money playing numbers. By the time you hit, you just getting back the money you put in.

**JOHNNY DOLLAR:** Numbers give poor black folks a chance. Same as if you take your money down there at Society for Savings. The bank give you a chance... a chance at interest. You may get more money back than you put in.

**SIX-FIVE:** If you can afford to leave it in there long enough.

**GIRLENA:** June Bailey up at 4 a.m. every morning figuring out what numbers he gonna play. Won't take a bath or brush his teeth 'til he get his numbers in. Won't eat 'til he get his numbers in. When he ever hit, Johnny Dollar?

**JOHNNY DOLLAR:** Ya gotta take a chance to win.

**SIX-FIVE:** June Bailey spend his whole disability check on numbers. I only play if I have a good dream.

**JOHNNY DOLLAR:** Good night, Irene.

**GIRLENA:** It's all right if you the lucky kind. If you got a feel for numbers. Play a little bit. Whatever June

Bailey dream about, he play. He look the number up in the dream book, play it, and the number don't fall. He play a number he see on a TV show and the number don't fall. He play the number he see on a cop car or on the side of the CTS.

**JOHNNY DOLLAR:** He taking a chance.

**GIRLENA:** I grew up around numbers. My whole family plays the numbers. I ain't never played a number in my life. Never. My Uncle William plays numbers so tough he keeps records of past numbers that fell on the backs of these old notebook pads. He's been recording numbers that fell for almost ten years. He studied trends and say he can predict when numbers will fall. Say playing numbers is a science, playing numbers is an art. A gift. Say he can read number patterns and predict when numbers will fall. My Uncle William plays numbers every day. Been playing numbers every day for twenty-five years. He ain't never hit for over twenty-five dollars in his life.

**SIX-FIVE:** My momma still collects the numbers for the entire block on 49$^{th}$. Don't mess with momma while she's watching her soap operas or working on her numbers. She gets a nice piece of every number that falls. She used to write numbers from Red John. Now she writes for Johnny Dollar.

**JOHNNY DOLLAR:** And she doing a real fine job… still. I learned numbers game from Red John. I used to cut school and run numbers for him. He drove a red Fleetwood with a coon tail on the back. He wore dark glasses, even in the winter. Said his eyes hurt him from writing so many numbers. Said his legs pained him from so much walking to pick up numbers. Used to walk with a gold plated cane. Red John died at the Massario Brother's numbers house. Red John screamed 736 at the top of his lungs and dropped dead. Folks said the red Fleetwood started up and went home without him the night he died. Said that Caddie was so used to leaving the number's house at 7 o'clock it left without him.

**GIRLENA:** Why don't you stop, Johnny Dollar.

**JOHNNY DOLLAR:** I ain't lying.

**SIX-FIVE:** I heard that same story from Leroy King.

**JOHNNY DOLLAR:** Good night, Irene.

**GIRLENA:** Don't encourage him, Six-Five.

**JOHNNY DOLLAR:** Red John was a legend around here.

**GIRLENA:** A legend in his own mind.

**JOHNNY DOLLAR:** I ain't lyin'.

**GIRLENA:** Please.

**JOHNNY DOLLAR:** Where can poor black folks get some extra cash? Yeah, you could shoot craps or get in a hot card game. You could sell some reefer, smack, or glue. Make your mark selling heroin or cocaine. A black man could put his bow legged woman out on the corner, or go out and rob the Sohio Gas Station on East 40$^{th}$, but why should he? He can play a number. If the number fall, he a winner. He back in the race.

**GIRLENA:** And if it don't fall?

**JOHNNY DOLLAR:** It might fall tomorrow.

**GIRLENA**: Or next week, or next month, *OR NEXT YEAR*... while he playing another number that don't fall. He better take that little piece of money and pay his rent or his light bill.

**JOHNNY DOLLAR:** Numbers give poor black folks an opportunity. I didn't start eating catfish at Art's Seafood 'til 336 fell in the old stock. Didn't own a Fleetwood 'til 829 fell in the big bond. 432 and triple fours got me twenty new suits and ten pair of snake skin shoes. Numbers put Johnny Dollar back in the race.

**SIX-FIVE:** Sometimes I play if I feel it. I've hit the number big. I've hit it small. I've busted the bank and there's been times I didn't get a dime.

**JOHNNY DOLLAR:** Sometimes you eat the bear; sometimes the bear eat you.

**GIRLENA:** Well, I'm gonna hold on to my paycheck and my tips. The Massario Brothers can get rich off some other poor black folks. It won't be Girlena Chatman.

**JOHNNY DOLLAR:** How you think the Allen twins bought the mansion on Liberty Boulevard?

**GIRLENA:** The Allen twins live in the Edna Hopper Nursing Home on 55th.

**JOHNNY DOLLAR:** The Allen twins used to own the Rockefeller Mansion on Liberty Boulevard.

**GIRLENA:** Johnny Dollar!

**JOHNNY DOLLAR:** I ain't lying. When they were cashiers at Giant Tiger on 83rd and Euclid the Big Twin hit that 036 for five thousand dollars on Monday and the next day the Lil' Twin hit that 541 in the Big Bond for seven thousand dollars. They bought the property from ole man Rockefeller for twelve thousand dollars the next week.

**GIRLENA:** What happened, Johnny Dollar? Why they living in a nursing home now?

**JOHNNY DOLLAR**: Twins said it was bad paper work.

**GIRLENA:** Bad paper work?

**JOHNNY DOLLAR:** Ole Man Rockefeller tricked 'em. Yeah, they said he was hooked up somehow some way with the Massario Family. Said Rockefeller really sold 'em some run down store front property on 49th for they twelve thousand dollars. They couldn't read and was too cheap to hire a lawyer so the white man fooled 'em. They was back at Giant Tiger the next week. Top it off, the city claimed the store front property through eminent domain. Paid 'em five thousand for the property but said they owed ten thousand in back taxes. They spent six months in jail for tax evasion. Twins said you can't trust rich white folks and they schemes. Good night, Irene.

**GIRLENA:** Can't you ever tell the truth?

**JOHNNY DOLLAR**: I ain't lying.

**GIRLENA:** Please.

**JOHNNY DOLLAR:** Numbers put Two Chins Charley back in the race just last week. Tell her, Six-Five.

**SIX-FIVE:** You know Two Chins Charley. Live up on Lexington, 1725. He'd loaned Peter Hill two hundred dollars. Peter Hill paid Two Chins back half the money. He still owed him one hundred dollars. Soon after Peter Hill got killed on Green Court. Stabbed by the Tyler sisters for running his mouth during a crap game. Two Chins was plenty upset. Said Peter Hill's big mouth got him killed with his money still in his pocket. Made him wanna dig him up and kill him again. Anyways three days after his funeral at the House of Wills, Peter Hill came to him in a dream. Said he was sorry he didn't get a chance to pay him the rest of that two hundred dollars. Peter Hill wrote 923 in the sky with a long finger. When Two Chins got up the next morning he put five dollars on 923 in the big bond. When he pulled in around 6:30 p.m. He saw Johnny Dollar's Fleetwood parked in front of his house. He knew 923 had fell.

**JOHNNY DOLLAR:** I got out of the Fleetwood and handed Two Chins an envelope with twenty eight hundred dollars minus my cut.

**SIX-FIVE:** Two Chins said that was one sweet scene.

**JOHNNY DOLLAR:** Good night, Irene.

*("Girl (Why You Wanna Make Blue)" by Temptations plays as lights fade out.)*

# SCENE III

**Time:** Three Days later. Late afternoon.

**At Rise:**

*(Gabby sits on steps holding a basketball. She is a young girl of eleven. Jamaica Pearl enters wearing a very short and stunning red dress.)*

**PEARL:** Hey there, Gabby.

**GABBY:** Hey.

**PEARL:** Seen Mr. Johnny Dollar? Mr. Johnny Dollar been here? I missed him at Ethel B's and Dilly's.

**GABBY:** Johnny Dollar been at 2158 and gone.

**PEARL:** I was trying to catch him so I could get my man's numbers in. Now King Willie II gonna be all agitated, taking his agitation out on me.

**GABBY:** Walk down to Troy's. He may be down to Troy's. He'll be there 'til it's time to go up the hill. If he gone, Troy'll call your number in. The Massario Brothers let Troy call numbers in late. They won't do it for anyone else. They'll do it for Troy.

**PEARL:** Thanks. I'll walk down there. What you doing with that ball?

**GABBY:** What you doing without one?

**PEARL:** Girl, I used to play ball all the time with my brothers 'fore they got sent off to the joint. 'Fore they started robbing and shooting folks. I was young like you. I could shoot, too. You could ask 'em if they were still around. They used to let me play to make teams even, since it was three of them.

**GABBY:** Momma said you went to East Tech.

**PEARL:** I went to East Tech for one year. Had to go to work to help my momma. I used to go to all the games. My brother Billy Boy Harris played with June Bailey and them. Billy Boy was a bench warmer mostly, but being a bench warmer for East Tech was a good thing. Being a bench warmer for East Tech was something special. Even East Tech benchwarmers like my brother Billy Boy got respect. Sometimes when it's slow, I like to stop and watch them East Tech boys play in Central Playground. They can play, but they can't compare to what June Bailey and them did... ain't nobody never gonna see nothing like that long as you live. You like playing ball, huh?

**GABBY:** Yep. Folks 'round here call me a Tom Boy because I like to play. If they wasn't calling me a Tom Boy, they'd be calling me something else. I plan to keep on playing 'til I decide to stop. Folks on East 55th street just better get used to hearing this ball right here bouncing.

**PEARL:** Be your own woman, gal!

**GABBY**: I am. *(Pause)* Why do you do what you do?

**PEARL:** Do what?

**GABBY:** You know, let men have their way with you for money?

**PEARL:** *(Smiling)* It's what I do.

**GABBY:** But why? You so pretty. Everybody 'round here says so. Any man 'round here would want to marry you. Buy you a big house and a new car.

**PEARL:** Too many demons behind all this so-called beauty, gal. Any man look close he'll see 'em, too.

**GABBY:** You like it?

**PEARL:** I'm good at it.

**GABBY:** So King Willie II made you… ah …

**PEARL:** A whore? Don't need to be scared to say it, girl. I ain't ashamed of it. It ain't like you or anyone else on East 55th calling me something I'm not. I am a whore, like my mother and like my grandmother before her. That is my family tree. *(Pause)* And King Willie II didn't make me a whore. That was all my doing. We was out. We was together one night. He said he was in trouble and he asked me to help him out sorta --- help him get some monies together. Get some monies together the fastest way I could… so I did that night. I kept going out each night helping him 'til he paid his debt to them Italians. I had been out on the street for three weeks before I honestly realized what I was doing. I was a whoring. *(Pause)* Besides, I loved him. Thought he was gonna marry me. Silly me. I sure found out different. And guess what? He had already paid his debt to the Massario Brothers. Didn't owe 'em a dime the first time he sent me out. He told me a year later when he got mad at me for something. He couldn't even remember what he was mad about. He told me that and then called me a DUMB…

**GABBY:** Why they call him King Willie II? Why don't folks just call him King Willie?

**PEARL:** He say his daddy was King Willie. He say he ain't his daddy. He say call him King Willie II.

**GABBY:** You love him? That's why you stay with him?

**PEARL:** Sometimes I feel love for him, sometimes I don't feel nothing.

**GABBY:** Why don't you leave?

**PEARL:** Where am I'm gonna go if I leave? King Willie II just like any other man on East 55th, I'd just have another pimp if I didn't have him. I'd be just some other pimp's whore. Another Pimps dumb ---

**GABBY:** But you don't have to be ah ....... ah whore. I don't know anyone 'round here prettier than you, Jamaica Pearl, 'cept my momma. All the men say ---

**PEARL:** *(Smiling)* Yeah, like some tall handsome gentleman is gonna come along on a white horse and carry me off to this big white castle.

**GABBY:** You need to stay ready so when he comes ---

**PEARL:** You dreaming, Chile.

**GABBY:** My momma said dreaming ain't a bad thing, long as you ain't dreaming foolishness, trying to catch a number like June Bailey.

**PEARL:** Or dreaming trying to catch a way off East 55th.

*(Girlena enters.)*

**GIRLENA:** Gabby, go in there and clean up that mess you left in my kitchen.

**GABBY:** You sure it was me?

**GIRLENA:** Please. Go on.

*(Gabby exits.)*

**PEARL:** Hey, Girlena.

**GIRLENA:** Hey, Girl. Hope she wasn't asking too many questions. She think she grown.

**PEARL:** *(Pause)* We talk all the time. Gabby reminds me a lot of myself when I was her age. *(Pause)* She asked me why I was a whore.

**GIRLENA:** I'm sorry. I'll talk to ---

**PEARL:** Girl, don't. I get asked that same question all the time. Usually from some lame or square John who claims he wants to marry me, set me free, give me babies, and make me a housewife.

**GIRLENA:** Or some lame or square drunk on a bar stool who claims he wants to make me one.

**PEARL:** At least your job is legitimate.

**GIRLENA:** Please. How's King Willie II?

**PEARL:** *(Pause)* He's changing little by little every day. He's started using his product. Lots of mood swings.

He added a couple more girls, which I don't mind, but now he's more demanding than ever, and completely obsessed with money. Never matters how much we bring in; it's never enough. He's never satisfied. *(Pause)* He's started to get mean. Real quick to use his fists now. King Willie II was never like that. He was always so sweet... gentle...

**GIRLENA:** What you gonna do?  You gotta do something, girl.

**PEARL:** I ain't gonna do nothing.

**GIRLENA:** It's only gonna get worse. *(Pause)* My momma took all those beatings from my daddy. *(Pause)* He almost sent her to her grave before the devil sent him to his. I said not me. Never. The first time a man puts his hands on me ---

**PEARL:** I am Red Delilah's daughter. You remember. Red Delilah was legendary. She worked East 55th... and Dilly's. Mr. Sweet was her pimp. Mr. Sweetside. She looked like a model *(Pause)* but she was just a whore. One of the best moneymakers to ever hit East 55th, everyone says. Red Delilah broke tradition. She was a contradiction of what East 55th whores were back then. Full figured, loud, boisterous. Red Delilah had light hazel eyes, yellow toned skin, wore her hair down her back in a single long silky pony tail. Moved like a dancer, a ballerina, on incredible legs, tapering down to small ankles and feet. Looked like a Jamaican Princess. When Red Delilah walked East 55th Street the men, young and old, black and white, took notice and, more often than not, walked single file behind her. Ain't no one 'round here since attracted a procession like that. Red Delilah was simply gorgeous. Many of the same features she passed on to me, her physical features and some deeper ones, the same features and the same demons …. I didn't even cry when they called to say Mr. Sweetside had killed my momma. She told me two weeks before he was gonna kill her ……

**GIRLENA:** Leave. Walk away. You can't ---

**PEARL:** If I left, King Willie II would ---

**GIRLENA:** He may anyway.

**PEARL:** If he find out I been seeing Mr. Sweetside.

**GIRLENA:** Jamaica Pearl! No! No!

**PEARL:** The same man who killed Red Delilah.

**GIRLENA:** *(Pause)* But ---

**PEARL:** It's alright. Mr. Sweetside said he was real sorry. Said he didn't mean to kill her.

**GIRLENA:** Girl you can't ---

**PEARL:** Gotta go. See if I can catch Mr. Johnny Dollar at Mr. Troy's and put these numbers in for King Willie II.

**GIRLENA:** You be careful, Jamaica Pearl. You be careful out here in these streets… and at home. Jamaica Pearl! Jamaica Pearl! You hear me?

*(Jamaica Pearl exits and lights fade to black as "Get Ready" by the Temptations plays.)*

# SCENE IV

**Time:** One week later. Friday 6:00 p.m.

**At Rise:**

*(A light breeze. The downstairs windows to 2158 are open. June Bailey, Six-Five, and Ricks sit at card table playing cards, drinking beer, and singing. Jimmy Love has nodded out.)*

**JUNE BAILEY/RICKS/SIX-FIVE:** *(Singing)*
*We are the Scarabs,*
*The Mighty Mighty Scarabs,*
*Everywhere we go,*
*People wanna know,*
*Who we are,*
*So we tell 'em,*

*We are the Scarabs,*
*The Mighty Mighty Scarabs,*
*When we hit the flo'*
*We put on a show!*

*(Laughing)*

**SIX-FIVE:** It was billed as the high school game of the century. The biggest event in schoolboy sports. Everybody and they momma was at the game.

**RICKS:** The morning of the game Fred Harris went down to the print shop and asked Mr. Weigand if he could print up a sign for good luck. The sign read TECH CAN'T LOSE! He punched two holes in it, got some ribbon from the girls in Home Economics and put it around his neck. Everyone saw the sign and wanted one. He had to go back down to the print shop. Fred Harris printed up sixteen hundred signs. By afternoon everyone in the school was wearing one. Students, teachers, teachers' assistants, janitors, EVERYONE. He even made a hand written poster of the same sign and took it to the game.

**SIX-FIVE:** Miss Ross and Mrs. Brister musta' had a hundred boosters in white gloves and white tops at the John Adams game that night. We played the game at Case Tech up on Euclid Avenue.

**RICKS:** It was close to two hundred and fifty boosters cheering at that Adams game. It was on a Friday night in early December. Who can ever forget that night?

**JUNE BAILEY:** All the Alpha Centurions and Nobles were there.

**RICKS:** All the Garcon Fillions and Laissez Fillions were there, too. School clubs were there, big back then. Everyone had on them club sweaters.

**SIX-FIVE:** The game was played at the college, because of the huge demand for tickets. Everyone wanted a ticket to that game. John Adams came in with a perfect record of 7-0. They had scored 100 points in every game.

**RICKS:** Adams had Leroy Cotton Robinson and Garland Stallworth. They were both All East Senate.

**JUNE BAILEY:** They had Arthur Finley and John Henderson, too. Them boys had some game.

**SIX-FIVE:** We were also 7-0 but had not yet hit the century mark. The Case Tech gym was packed. Three Thousand strong! Standing room only. Fire Marshalls had to turn hundreds of folks away. Man, the roar of the crowd was deafening as we ran out the locker room through a line formed by our cheerleaders.

**RICKS:** Fine cheerleaders.

**SIX-FIVE:** The li'l mascot was little DeWayne. He led us out. The *two hundred and fifty* boosters in white tops and white gloves rose as one on Mrs. Ross's signal. In the pre-game huddle, Coach Chavers talked about who we were, and how we were, not only playing for our school, but playing for our community, as well. It was middle class affluent kids from Lee-Harvard vs. the poor kids from the projects. The "have-nots" vs. the "haves," he said. Just before the jump ball I looked up at the top of the gym, and someone had hung a sign. *TECH CAN'T LOSE.* We were up by eleven at the half.

**RICKS:** We led all the way.

**JUNE BAILEY:** We beat John Adams 75-66! The next day the headlines of the Sports Section in the Cleveland Press read *"Mighty Scarabs Whoop it up on Gloomy Night for Adams Family."*

**SIX-FIVE:** Adams did have the better team that year. We just didn't believe anyone could beat us.

**RICKS:** And no one did. All Coach Chavers had to do was throw the balls out! Just throw the balls out!

**SIX-FIVE:** Cause Tech Can't Lose! Somebody took the sign down after the game and hung in the gym. It's still hanging there. You know who was the Chairman of the Boards!

**JUNE BAILEY:** I scored twenty from all over.

**RICKS:** I had sixteen. Fast Eddie Cain had eleven. Jimmy Love had fourteen. Remember, Jimmy? Jimmy? Jimmy?

**SIX-FIVE:** *(Shaking him)* Wake up, fool. Wake up.

**LOVE:** What? Huh? Who's turn?

**SIX-FIVE:** Your turn. I had twenty-two rebounds. I made the Plain Dealer Dream Team that week.

**JUNE BAILEY:** Took you long enough. You was the last one to make it.

**LOVE:** *(Playing with cap)* Jimmy Love was the first. Twenty-six points against Cathedral Latin. Twenty-Two against East High. I was riding high back then.

**SIX-FIVE:** You still *are.*

**RICKS:** You need to stop nodding out, boy, and pay attention! We talking about history here.

**LOVE:** You'll know I'm paying attention after the beating I'ma give y'all.

**RICKS:** You dreaming, boy. With the hand I got here, I'm gonna turn your dreams into nightmares.

**JUNE BAILEY:** What time is it? Who's got the time?

**SIX-FIVE:** 6 p.m.

**RICKS:** Why you worrying about time?

**SIX-FIVE:** June Bailey finally back in the race.

**JUNE BAILEY:** Time is money. Money is time. Hear what I say?

**RICKS:** You got plenty time. What you ain't got is a love life.

**JUNE BAILEY:** Why he talkin' 'bout himself, Junior?

**SIX-FIVE:** Maybe he talking about Mr. Jimmy Love over there?

**LOVE:** I know he ain't talking about Mr. Jimmie Love. Mr. Jimmie Love got a sweet life. Things changed, man. Things ain't what they used to be. But me and that "boy," that "smack," that smooth and mellow, we doing just fine. He's my ride or die now. *(Laughs)* Ride. Or Die.

**RICKS:** What?

**LOVE:** Y'all heard me. Nothing can compete with mixing heroin with cocaine, it's what they call Speedballing, and believe me there ain't nothing on God's earth feels better than BALLING with a lot of SPEED!

**JUNE BAILEY:** That white boy done cost this poor boy his mind.

**SIX-FIVE:** He stone nuts.

**LOVE:** I'm telling you, that white boy is where it's at.

**RICKS:** When Killer get here?

**JUNE BAILEY:** Real soon I hear. They lettin' him out early for good behavior.

**SIX-FIVE:** Good behavior? He gotta be fooling somebody.

**LOVE:** What a lame.

**RICKS:** Big Dumb.

**SIX-FIVE:** I never seen a fool who wanted to play for East Tech so bad and couldn't play.

**JUNE BAILEY:** Couldn't play a lick.

**RICKS:** Ain't many sports you can play with two left feet. What Girlena gonna do when Killer get here?

**SIX-FIVE:** Say she may go up to Chicago.

**JUNE BAILEY:** *(Shouting)* Girlena! Girlena! Ricks wanna know what you gonna do when Killer get here?

**RICKS:** Man, don't ---

**JUNE BAILEY:** I know what I'ma do when Johnny Dollar gets here.

*(Girlena appears at downstairs window.)*

**GIRLENA:** What you want, June Bailey? I'm trying to cook y'all some chicken. You didn't wanna talk to me earlier when you was writing your numbers this morning.

**JUNE BAILEY:** *(Smiling)* Ricks wondering if you wanna join us in a game of Whist? He need a partner.

**GIRLENA:** Ricks ain't asked me to be his partner. Anyway, y'all ain't gonna keep me up all night with y'all Negro buffoonery.

**JUNE BAILEY:** We jus' wanna look at them pretty bow legs. Get somethin' started. Hear what I say?

**GIRLENA:** Please. Y'all have a better chance of getting' something started with them Allen twins.

**JUNE BAILEY:** Allen twins gotta be close to seventy.

**LOVE:** Seventy-Five.

**GIRLENA:** That's about all y'all can handle. Hear what I say?

*(Exits through window.)*

**JUNE BAILEY:** I hear ya.

**SIX-FIVE:** By the time Killer get here, I'll be in Iowa. Got a Chicago stop, and then I'll be heading due west.

**JUNE BAILEY:** See, Six-Five a smart man. Six-Five shufflin' out while the shufflin' is good.

**RICKS:** What you hauling, Six-Five?

**SIX-FIVE:** Twenty-five thousand pair of black fish net stockings.

**RICKS:** I'd love to see Girlena in a pair of those.

**JUNE BAILEY:** Save him a pair, Six-Five. He can look at 'em and dream about Girlena wearin 'em.

**RICKS:** Ain't gonna do no dreaming.

**JUNE BAILEY:** Woooo! Oh, he talkin' tough now. Maybe he gonna finally go after his first love. *(Yelling)* Girlena! Girlena!

**RICKS:** Come on, June Bailey.

*(Girlena appears in lower window.)*

**GIRLENA:** June Bailey, you better stop bothering me if you want this chicken fried.

**JUNE BAILEY:** Get that little black dress ready. We going to Leo's Casino to see the Temptations tomorrow night. June Bailey gonna get you a backstage pass, too. We gonna rent a white Cadillac. We gonna rent a white Cadillac, get white boy in a white suit and let him drive.

**GIRLENA:** Please.

**JUNE BAILEY:** We going to Leo's Casino championship style. We gonna be big time, like we were in '55. Hear what I say?

**GIRLENA:** You must be drunk.

*(Girlena exits.)*

**JUNE BAILEY:** Drunk? *(Yelling)* Just get that little black dress ready, Girlena. Show off them pretty bow legs. Get somethin' started.

**SIX-FIVE:** You makin' your move on Girlena before Killer get here, June Bailey?

**JUNE BAILEY:** Girlena sent me packin' back in elementary school. I'ma get them tickets and a backstage pass and Ricks gonna take her.

**LOVE:** Girlena gonna be his White Lady.

**RICKS:** What you talking about, June Bailey?

**JUNE BAILEY:** You gotta have a game plan, Ricks. Ever since elementary school you always had my back. You always been looking out for me. June Bailey got your back this time.

**RICKS:** Girlena ain't gonna go to Leo's Casino with me.

**JUNE BAILEY:** Don't you know nothing? Girlena love her some Temptations. She got all they 45's and albums. She ain't gonna miss seein' The Temptations. Get your red zoot suit ready. It'll go real nice with that little black dress. You can even borrow my new red straw hat, but you gonna have to get the Verde red snake skin shoes from Johnny Dollar.

**SIX-FIVE:** June Bailey got a good game plan, Ricks.

**LOVE:** That's where it's at, baby!

**RICKS:** I don't know.

**JUNE BAILEY:** I know. Ricks always been crazy about Girlena, since elementary school. He jus' didn't know how to get to her, and circumstances never allowed him the opportunity. June Bailey gonna give him that... the opportunity. *(Pause)* Girlena like you,

Ricks. She done said as much, but she the kinda chick you gotta push up on. She'll keep right on movin' if you don't. Until you push up on her, tell her what you want, or she'll keep right on goin'. You still in the game. Besides, you only got a few days 'fore Killer get here. Then it's ---

**SIX-FIVE:** *(Laughing)* Game over.

**JUNE BAILEY:** If you don't push it ain't gonna happen. You gonna always be in the back of the line ...back of the bus... back of the room. You gotta push. Just a little push ...a little push today... a little push tomorrow ... before long you done pushed your way through... pushed your way in... Sometimes you push when a woman ain't looking... if you careful, sometimes you push while she looking... just a little push...so she really ain't sure if you pushin'... hell, sometimes she may know you pushin' and that's alright... That's the beauty of it... she gonna be pushin', too.

**SIX-FIVE**: All y'all better push before Killer gets here.

**RICKS:** Everybody ain't scared of Killer.

**LOVE:** All y'all better be. Killer ain't never liked none of y'all East Tech basketball playing niggers.

**JUNE BAILEY:** Let June Bailey take care of this, Ricks.

**SIX-FIVE:** *(Pause)* Remember that fight in junior high school? Eddie Cain and Killer were trying to kill each other over Girlena.

**JUNE BAILEY:** Killer know Girlena stayed at your crib for a while when he was in the joint.

**SIX-FIVE:** That's a fact.

**JUNE BAILEY:** Killer may have a problem with that.

**SIX-FIVE:** If he do, he can see me when I come back from Iowa.

**JUNE BAILEY:** If he the same old Killer, he will see you. Hear what I say?

**SIX-FIVE:** I sure ain't running.

**JUNE BAILEY:** Loan Six-Five one of your duelin' pistols, Ricks.

**RICKS:** I may need both pistols to cover your ass, June Bailey. Hear what I say?

**JUNE BAILEY:** Y'all sure are some funny characters.

*(Johnny Dollar enters from right.)*

**JUNE BAILEY:** Johnny Dollar. Jus' the man June Bailey wanna see. Been waiting on you since the 5 o'clock news. June Bailey got that 247 straight for five dollars in the big bond. The big bond is the only way to play. Hear what I say? June Bailey on his way to Mike the Hatter and get that powder blue straw hat. Then June Bailey gonna do Rosenbloom's and get a powder blue shallow-stripe sharkskin three piece suit. Next boys, June Bailey headed for Regal Shoes and get a pair of powder blue snakeskin shoes.

**JOHNNY DOLLAR:** Look... ah... June Bailey. *(Pause)* Look, they cut the number. They cut it five ways. They ain't paying but five hundred dollars. The Massario Brothers ain't paying but five hundred dollars on 247.

**JUNE BAILEY:** What? I know you ain't come here talkin' what you talkin'.

**JOHNNY DOLLAR:** They ain't paying but five hundred dollars, June Bailey.

**LOVE:** Damn.

**SIX-FIVE:** They do it every time.

**JOHNNY DOLLAR:** The Massario Brothers ain't paying but five hundred dollars. The number cut. The Massario Brothers done cut that number five ways. I'm sorry. I had three dollars on the number myself.

**JUNE BAILEY:** *(Rising)* I woke up this mornin', I ain't had but ten dollars. Ten dollars left from my disability check. Ten dollars to my name. I call you and say, "Johnny Dollar put ten dollars on 247." Put ten dollars on 247 and put it in the big bond, 'cause I feel lucky. Put it in the big bond 'cause I want big cash. I want big monies. You say, "Why 247, June Bailey?" I say, I dreamed of making love to this bow legged woman all night at the Alcazar Hotel in room 247. You say Okay. You come down here to 2158 and get June Bailey's last ten dollars. The last ten dollars to my name. I tell you June Bailey feeling real good about 247. Real good. Ain't felt this good since **'45.** Been playing that 247 for a year. 365 days. Give them Massario Brothers a lotta money... lotta money since I been playing that number. When the Cleveland Press final edition come out, I see June Bailey's number fell, 247 straight! When the five o'clock news come out it say 247. Say 247 Straight. June Bailey got five thousand dollars. June Bailey's ship finally come in. June Bailey back in the race. Call all my friends over. We celebrating. We playin' cards, drinkin' beer, shootin' the shit, Girlena fryin' up tons of chicken… she got French fries popping in fresh Crisco… Ricks cheatin' and Slim Slim winnin' all the damn hands. I even got something for you, Johnny Dollar. Got a bottle of your favorite gin. Now you stroll in here like you walkin' in the park, and tell me that The Massario Brothers ain't payin' but five hundred dollars? Ain't payin' but five hundred dollars, 'cause everybody and they momma including you, Johnny Dollar, decided to play June Bailey's damn number, 247 instead of playing their own. And them white folks is driving Fleetwoods and living large and good up and down Little Italy, and you driving a Fleetwood and livin' out on the Gold Coast, wearing silk suits, Verde snake skin shoes, a Stetson hat, and they all gonna come in handy when old man Wills have to dress your ass for the last time. Where's the rest of my damn money, nigger?

**JOHNNY DOLLAR:** I ain't lying.

**JUNE BAILEY:** Well somebody might be dyin' tonight. Me and Ricks gonna ride up that hill and see them Massario Brothers.

**JOHNNY DOLLAR:** Don't do that, June Bailey. Y'all gonna get hurt real bad. Them white folks don't play.

**JUNE BAILEY:** They gonna find out June Bailey don't play, just like they found out in '55.

**JOHNNY DOLLAR:** This ain't no game they playing. This is real. This is real life. Now I know you mad, June Bailey. Lotta black folks mad tonight. Lotta parties and celebrations postponed... cancelled. They mad on Lexington and Hough. They mad on Kinsman. They mad on Superior and St. Clair. They mad on Central. They mad up and down Cedar. It ain't my fault, June Bailey. If I had my way I would pay all those mad black folks. I'd pay you your Five Thousand dollars. I just do what I'm told. It's just a job, June Bailey. I ain't gonna take no heat for doing my job. And I can't pay all these mad black folks out of my pocket. Roland Massario called me, He say, "Johnny Dollar, 247 is cut five ways." He say, "Come get your hits, and pay your people." I say Okay.

**JUNE BAILEY:** Give me my five hundred dollars, nigger.

**JOHNNY DOLLAR**: *(Handing him the money)* Them folks don't play, June Bailey.

**JUNE BAILEY:** Neither do we. Ricks, got your 38?

**RICKS:** *(Rising)* You know it. Shotgun at the house.

**JUNE BAILEY:** We'll stop and get it on our way. Six-Five, tell Girlena we be back. Tell her to save me a couple chicken legs.

*(June Bailey and Ricks exit as lights fade to black. "Ball of Confusion" plays.)*

## ACT II

"Baby, if you live, your time will come ..."

**Blues Theme**

### SCENE V

**Time:** Two days later, Noon

**At Rise:**

*(Gabby stands near basketball hoop. She takes the basketball between her legs and behind her back at a furious pace. She stops and crosses to table to sit as "Fading Away" by The Temptations fades out.)*

**DJ:** Turn up the volume
Dig on the beat,
Grab a bow legged woman
And shuffle your feet,
Just like racecar rolls around the track,
Uncle Paul plays all the hits
Back to back to back,

Alright, Uncle Paul got an announcement. Friday night I want the whole city of Cleveland to meet down at Leo's Casino at 9 p.m. We gonna have a red "Miniskirt and Miss Bow Legs" contest. Uncle Paul gonna be there spinnin' the jams. Our Program Director, Hot Tina gonna be there, and Tina say she gonna give it away to some lucky young guy, and everybody know when Tina get hot the whole city of Cleveland gonna be smoking, baby so get on down to Leo's Casino, that's Friday night at 9 o'clock. Are you ready to jam? I am. On this Temptations' weekend on 890 AM WKMU. Cleveland, Ohio. The sooooooul of the city, baby.

*("I Wish it Would Rain" starts to play. Gabby rises and turns radio down.)*

**GABBY:** I hate that song.

*(Ricks enters from carrying bag of mail.)*

**RICKS:** I love that song. *(Singing)*
Sunshine, Blue Sky
Please go away.

**GABBY:** Ugh. I hate it even more now.

**RICKS:** *(To mail boxes)* I'll remember that on your birthday and Christmas.

**GABBY:** You'll have to send my gifts to Chicago.

**RICKS:** *(Placing mail in boxes)* Chicago?

**GABBY:** Yep.

**RICKS:** *(To her)* Why Chicago?

**GABBY:** Mom's saying we going to Chicago. Live with my Aunt Betty for a while. She won't say why. Said I was born there. Something's going on, and Gabriella Chatman is gonna find out.

**RICKS:** *(Pause)* I'm sure she has her reasons. Mothers always do. She inside?

**GABBY:** She went down to the Greyhound with Six-Five.

**RICKS:** You by yourself?

**GABBY:** Might as well be. June Bailey in there staring at the wall.

**RICKS:** He is, huh? Johnny Dollar been here?

**GABBY:** Naw. June Bailey told Johnny Dollar to stay away from 2158. I can't believe June Bailey ain't playing numbers no more. That's crazy. Hear what I say? He don't even wanna shoot baskets anymore. June Bailey is a real drag these days. I may as well go to Chicago. Who I'm gonna play?

**RICKS:** You still play with the boys 'round here?

**GABBY:** They all the time be squawking, 'cause I can beat most of 'em. They either squawking or they trying to hurt me. Ever since Eddie... *(Pause)* and June Bailey don't come up there anymore...the boys try to knock me down when I drive to the basket, so now I jus' shoot over 'em now. Ball usually don't touch nothing but net. Swish... Sometimes I hit the rim if I want to. It's not good to show off like y'all did in '55. I was looking at the old newspaper clipping just the other day. Y'all used to always say after a win, here we go dancin'.

**RICKS:** *(Smiling)* Here we go dancing.

**GABBY:** Momma said y'all owned this city back then.

**RICKS:** We all had keys to the city. We ate at the Lancer Steak House before every Friday night game. Someone or some group always sponsored the meal. They sat with the team, asked for autographs, and took pictures. We had to wear white shirts and ties. Everyone wore the gold East Tech Blazer with the Scarab emblem on the handkerchief pocket.

**GABBY:** Choice.

**RICKS:** We played all our big games at Case Tech. We played at the City Championship at the Cleveland Arena. East Senate versus the West Senate. The City Championship was never much of a game. Just ask West Tech. *(Pause)* They used to play the Harlem Globetrotters' theme song when we came out.

**GABBY:** Sweet Georgia Brown.

*(Gabby and Ricks start to whistle the song.)*

**RICKS:** There you go girl. Coach Chavers used to play for the Globe Trotters and he started that. Before a game we never came out first. We did that to get inside the other team's head. We wait 'til the last minute, and then we come out and the crowd would go crazy.

**GABBY:** Double and triple crazy, Mom said.

**RICKS:** Never had to take the bus. If I needed to go somewhere, I just stood on the corner of East 55th with my brown and gold East Tech gym bag. Someone always stopped. Say, "You play for East Tech?" I say, "Yeah" in a cool voice. They say, "Come on. Hop in."

**GABBY:** So choice.

**RICKS:** *(Pause)* I been thinking lately maybe it wasn't so choice.

**GABBY:** Why? You guys are heroes. Folks in the neighborhood still talk about y'all like it just happened yesterday. Every afternoon Troy's be full of folks talking politics, and still talking 'bout '55. Troy's got all the old photos and clippings up all over the store. Troy said it was the only thing the community had to be proud of back then. Said y'all even gave poor folks a chance to be winners. Troy be telling folks how he was in Columbus. He drove down in a snowstorm. It took him seven hours to get there. Everybody say y'all were heroes.

**RICKS** Being heroes may have doomed some of us.

**GABBY**: But how?

**RICKS:** *(Placing mailbag on table and crossing slowly to basket)* After Championship season of '55 the entire community embraced us. Placed us on pedestals and made us... heroes... we could do no wrong. We were heroes... heroes... of which the community had never known. We were given everything. We were denied nothin'. The community covered over each and every mistake we made. Conveniently looking the other way... denying our youthful indiscretions... East 55th was jus' a little piece of the world. Jus' a little piece of the world... where we played... where we slow-danced across each day with no real responsibility, accountability, or reason... it became a paradise of sorts. A paradise where we were locked in... grounded... which turned out to be forever... never realizing who we were or our real worth outside this paradise... We were trapped... isolated... unaware of the world outside... never venturing out to seek opportunities... afraid of exploring possibilities beyond... this little piece of the world.

**GABBY:** But everyone talks about '55.

*(Lights dim to a blue hue.)*

**RICKS:** '55. We were the first Black high school in Ohio to win the state championship in basketball. The only school black or white from Cleveland to win it all. No one can ever deny us that. No one can ever take that from us. We surprised them white folks down in Columbus. They weren't ready for us. The St. John Arena on the campus of Ohio State University ain't never seen nothing like us. June Bailey and Fast Eddie Cain scoring. Me and Six-Five reboundin'. Jimmy Love and Paul Bell who could run, jump, and play defense. Old Coach Chavers had a squad. All he had to do was throw the balls out. Ohio State University, St. John's Arena in Columbus, Ohio. The Ohio Class Double AA High School Basketball State Championship Game.

*(Background noise of a high school basketball game can be heard.)*

**GABBY:** Eighteen Seconds left on the clock. This is East Tech's last chance. Right here. Right now. June Bailey to inbound. Quick pass to Ricks on the right wing. Ricks dribbles left, inside to Junior Payne, back out to Jimmy Love, across to Fast Eddie Cain at the top of the key. Fast Eddie Cain passes to June Bailey, June Bailey dribbles left, spins, gets by his defender in the lane, ball in the air. Everyone on their feet... Swish. Buzzer. Game over! Game over!

**GABBY/RICKS:** Here we go dancin'...

**RICKS:** *(Smiling)* That's how we won it! That's just how it happened.

**GABBY:** June Bailey used to play the tape of that radio broadcast every night. He don't play it anymore.

**RICKS:** You only surprise white folks once. They're ready for you the next time you come around. Ain't no black school won since. They go down, but they come back empty. What we did in '55 was great. Great for the school. The community. The City. '55 just carried a heavy price tag... and some of us are still paying it.

**GABBY:** Think they'll let girls play for their school one day?

**RICKS:** I think it's coming. Everybody's talking about Civil Rights. Female Rights can't be too far behind, huh?

*(Girlena enters carrying a bag of groceries.)*

**GABBY:** Where's Six-Five?

**GIRLENA:** He had to make a run. Put this chicken in the 'fridge.

**GABBY:** *(Taking bags and crossing to entrance.)* Want me to wash 'em?

**GIRLENA:** You trying to impress somebody?

**GABBY:** Here we go dancin'.

*(Gabby exits.)*

**GIRLENA:** That child. *(Pause)* Any mail?

**RICKS:** *(Sitting)* In your box. *(Pause)* I couldn't help but notice a letter from Killer.

**GIRLENA:** *(To mailbox and retrieving mail)* He's been writing recently.

**RICKS:** Had a Cleveland postmark.

**GIRLENA:** Probably sent it to his mother and she forwarded it to 2158.

**RICKS:** Gabby said you're leaving?

**GIRLENA:** *(To him)* Pretty much planned to do that. Yep.

**RICKS:** Chicago?

**GIRLENA:** Chicago… again. Different circumstances this time, though.

**RICKS:** How you getting up there?

**GIRLENA:** Greyhound. I always wanted to ride that double-decker bus. I really don't feel like dealing with Killer.

**RICKS:** *(Pause)* I could run you up to Chicago. I start my two-week vacation after today.

**GIRLENA:** Please. You know you don't wanna be bothered with me and Gabby all the way to Chicago.

**RICKS:** I would do it, Girlena.

**GIRLENA:** *(Laughing)* You gonna talk to me, Ricks? Chicago's a long trip, and you ain't gonna talk to a girl.

**RICKS:** I figured you'd want to listen to the radio, some Marvin Gaye or the Temptations?

**GIRLENA:** That's okay, but, really, I like a man to talk to me.

**RICKS:** I can never get my thoughts together around you, Girlena.

**GIRLENA:** You didn't even talk to me the entire time we were at Leo's Casino.

**RICKS:** I couldn't find the right words to say. You looked... you looked ---

**GIRLENA:** You liked the dress, Ricks?

**RICKS:** Everything.

**GIRLENA:** Please.

**RICKS:** The icing on the cake was when we went backstage, and you were dancing with the Temptations. It reminded me of those days back at Tech when y'all used to hand dance in the cafeteria during recess.

**GIRLENA:** God. Recess used to be so much fun back then. Why watch ten or fifteen minutes of a lame movie in the auditorium when you could dance to the latest 45s? Why didn't you ever dance, Ricks?

**RICKS:** I just enjoyed watching you.

**GIRLENA:** Please. *(Smiling)* Never learned how, huh?

**RICKS:** I knew how. I just preferred watching... you.

**GIRLENA:** Let's see.

*(Girlena crosses to radio and turns it on. She offers her hand to Ricks. He takes it as "My Girl" by the Temptations starts to play. Ricks and Girlena begin to hand dance to the music as the lights dim. They are precise and graceful, as though they have been partners all their lives, and perhaps, in many ways, they have. The song ends. They stand for a moment holding hands.)*

**GIRLENA:** What took you so long, Ricks?

**RICKS:** Just waiting for the right moment, I guess.

**GIRLENA:** Please. *(Whispering)* I think this might be it. What you think, Ricks?

*(They kiss.)*

**GIRLENA:** *(Crossing away)* Thank you for last night.

**RICKS:** My Pleasure.

**GIRLENA:** *(Sitting)* Meeting the Temptations was truly incredible. It was really sweet of June Bailey to get those tickets and that back stage pass after the Massario Brothers cut his number. He spent his entire hit on us.

**RICKS:** That's June Bailey. He's one of a kind.

**GIRLENA:** *(Pause)* What happened when you went to see the Massario Brothers?

**RICKS:** When we left East 55th we pretty much were out of touch with reality. Pretty much. On our way to my apartment to pick up the shotgun it dawned on me that we perhaps had not made a very wise decision. Pass on shotgun. I also came to the realization that riding through Little Italy in an old Ford pickup looking for the Massario Mansion could pose major problems. Pass on that idea. Nevertheless, feeling very much like heroes, we made a detour up the hill to the number's house on East Boulevard figuring to catch at least one of the Massario Brothers there. Roland Massario was there with his bodyguards. They let us in never checking for weapons. I guess they figured us to be strictly heroes of '55, and that we posed no danger. June Bailey asked Roland Massario for the rest of his money. He explained that he played 247 in good faith, and it was not his fault that other folks had decided 247 was a good hunch, and wrote a number on their number slips that he'd be playing for a year. At least four guns were drawn. I coulda pulled my gun, but that would have made matters worse. I wasn't sure what June Bailey was planning, but I knew this was nothing like '55, and I wasn't gonna ever see the age of 55. Roland Massario told his bodyguards to escort us out, and, having weighed our options, I was much obliged to do just that. He added to that if we ever made a trip back up Murray Hill, it would be our last trip. From his look and body language, he meant it. June Bailey was real silent as we left. I had a feeling he had planned to go out in a blaze of glory. On the way back he asked me if we were cowards. I told him no. I told him we were still heroes, but there was no point in being dead heroes... He said he would have to think on that, but he might take a ride back up Murray Hill one day to see the Massario Brothers. You know how he gets when something starts eating at him. He can't let it go. *(Pause)* He's going back up that hill one day, and when he does, I can't let him go alone.

**GIRLENA:** *(Softly)* I know.

**RICKS:** *(Pause)* When you planning on leaving, if you go?

**GIRLENA:** Early.

**RICKS:** I'll run you and Gabby up there.

**GIRLENA:** You gonna protect me, Ricks?

**RICKS:** *(Rising)* I'm gonna always do that.

**GIRLENA:** Please. You gonna talk to me?

**RICKS:** I can pretty much get my thoughts together now.

**GIRLENA:** Is that so?

**RICKS:** Yep.

**GIRLENA:** Call me. I'm sure you have the number, though you've never used it.

**RICKS:** *(Smiling)* Yep. I got your number.

*(Ricks exits as Gabby enters.)*

**GABBY:** Chicken's washed. Where Ricks go?

**GIRLENA:** Delivering the rest of his mail.

**GABBY:** After June Bailey, Rick's my favorite. He never had an outside shot though. *(Pause)* Mom, why wasn't Ricks ever your boyfriend? He's cool. He's smart. Ricks is fine.

**GIRLENA:** Gabriella Chatman.

**GABBY:** Mom, I'm only eleven but I know when a man is fine.

**GIRLENA:** Don't get yourself in trouble, little girl. *(Pause)* Don't select a man simply based on his looks. You have to find worth in other areas.

**GABBY:** Whenever Ricks talks about you, he gets that little twinkle in his eye.

**GIRLENA:** Please.

**GABBY:** June Bailey said Ricks been crazy about you since y'all were in elementary school. June Bailey said all the boys were. Said your legs always stopped traffic. Said when you walked you brought tears to the boys' eyes.

**GIRLENA:** June Bailey's been hanging around Johnny Dollar. He exaggerates the truth.

**GABBY:** *(Pause)* Is Eddie Cain my real daddy?

**GIRLENA:** Why would you ask me a silly question like that?

**GABBY:** Is he?

**GIRLENA:** What's going on with you, Gabriella Chatman?

**GABBY:** I've just been putting a few things together.

**GIRLENA:** What things?

**GABBY:** Things I remember. I never forget stuff.

**GIRLENA:** What stuff?

**GABBY:** When I was eight ---

**GIRLENA:** When you were eight?

**GABBY:** We were all at the playground shooting. Me, June Bailey, and Six-Five. June Bailey made five or six shots in a row. I shot after him. I made six in a row and Six-Five said, "Like father like daughter."

**GIRLENA:** Six-Five, June Bailey, and Ricks have always called you their daughter.

**GABBY:** He and Six-Five had strange looks on their faces after he said it.

**GIRLENA:** Please.

**GABBY:** When June Bailey came to my open house at school my teacher said your dad is nice. I asked her how she knew he was my dad? She said, "You look just like him. You even walk like him."

**GIRLENA:** People can see resemblances in anyone if they want to and they look hard enough.

**GABBY:** Last week Ms. Cook was in Troy's. It was crowded with the regulars. I was behind the meat counter. I heard Ms. Cook tell Mother White that you were messing with three or four guys when I was born. She said you didn't know who my daddy was. She said when Killer Davis comes home ---

**GIRLENA:** Ms. Cook is a nosy… I told you who your daddy is!

**GABBY:** It bothered me all day, so this morning I asked June Bailey if Eddie Cain was my daddy. He just looked at me. I asked him if he was my daddy. He walked away. Why didn't he answer me?

**GIRLENA:** June Bailey ain't been himself.

**GABBY:** June Bailey always answers my questions. I remember I asked him what a scarab was. He said it was an Egyptian beetle. *(Pause)* Who's my daddy, momma? Is it June Bailey? Is it Eddie Cain? Is it Six-Five? Killer?

**GIRLENA:** I told you who your daddy is, Gabby.

**GABBY:** *(Pause)* You don't know, do you, Momma? Ms. Cook was right.

**GIRLENA:** *(Shaking her)* I know who your daddy is. It's Eddie Cain. Eddie Cain. "Eddie Cain is my daddy." Say it. Say it. "Eddie Cain is my daddy."

**GABBY:** *(Crying)* Eddie Cain is my daddy. Eddie Cain is my daddy.

**GIRLENA:** Eddie Cain is your daddy. *(Pause.)* Ms. Cook should have come and asked me. A woman knows things like that. I know I made some bad choices when it came to men. I am my mother's daughter. The Chatman women, I think we were destined to choose the wrong men. Don't make our mistakes. *(Pause)* I watched my daddy hit my momma three or four times in her head with a hammer. Put her in the hospital for six months. The first day she came home she was in the kitchen trying to fix him his favorite food, chili and fried chicken. One week later he pushed her down six flights of stairs claiming she was cheating on him with Peter Hill. All the time he was cheating on her with Lilly Davis down the street. The best thing that happened to us --- he had a heart attack and died. Died at the kitchen table. Just dropped dead. I slept well that night. Didn't three people come to his funeral. Momma made me and my sister go. We made three. All the time I was with Eddie Cain, off and on I thought about my daddy, Carl Chatman. I thought about him. I asked myself was it wrong to love a bad person? Why did I love Eddie Cain? Why? I asked myself that same question about Killer before he shot Jackie Lee outside of Ellis Bar. I watched the police handcuff him and put him in the back of the police car. All the time he was screaming he killed Jackie Lee to protect me. *(Crying)* Jackie Lee tipped his hat and smiled. That's what southern men do. He was asking me how to get to Western Auto on 83rd and Euclid. He'd just come up here from Alabama. He was married with two small kids. Come up here looking for a job and went back in a box because some man I was seeing was too stupid to understand the man was just being polite, being a gentleman. *(Pause)* Killer was yelling he killed Jackie Lee to protect me. Protect me? Protect Me? Protect me from what? Yelling I better wait for him. He'd wait for me... he'd wait for me... forever

*(Jamaica Pearl enters slowly carrying an old cap.)*

**PEARL:** Hey, Girlena, where's June Bailey?

**GIRLENA:** He in there still staring at that blank wall. Why? What's wrong?

**PEARL:** *(Handing cap to her)* See they just discovered Jimmy Love and Big Edgar dead on a rooftop on East 49th. They been up there for a few days. They OD'd off some heroin Mr. Walter brought in from New York. Now every junkie on East 55th looking to score from Mr. Walter before the cops catch up with him. They saying the heroin Mr. Walter got is top shelf. Sends you to a high-life. Sends you on a wild, wild trip. The wildest trip folks on East 55th seen in a long time. Now ain't this world jus' crazy?

*("Try to Remember" plays as Jamaica Pearl exits and lights fade out.)*

## SCENE VI

**Time:** 8 p.m. One week later.

**At Rise:**

*(Lightning and thunder as a summer storm moves towards the area.)*

*(Killer Davis enters. He is a Black man in his early thirties. He crosses to apartment entrance and begins to knock. When there is no response he knocks harder.)*

**KILLER:** Girlena! Girlena! *(Crossing to downstairs window)* Hey, Girlena! It's Killer. I'm home, baby. Let me in. Girlena!

*(June Bailey enters from apartment and stops on porch steps.)*

**JUNE BAILEY:** Welcome home, Killer.

**KILLER:** June Bailey. As I live and breathe. I didn't expect you to be a member of the welcoming committee, since I wasn't one of the heroes of '55. *(Pause)* Where's Girlena?

**JUNE BAILEY:** She's gone, Killer.

**KILLER:** Gone where?

**JUNE BAILEY:** Not sure. Maybe with her aunt in Alabama. Maybe with her sister in Kentucky. She didn't say.

**KILLER:** She got my letters. She knew I was coming home.

**JUNE BAILEY:** She never mentioned it.

**KILLER:** So you say.

**JUNE BAILEY:** She put her notice in two weeks ago.

**KILLER:** She been working at Ellis Bar since she turned legal. She help run that place now. She just gonna just up and leave?

**JUNE BAILEY:** Maybe she wanted something better. Like most of us, she been on East 55th all her life.

**KILLER:** Everything you want is right within your grasp. If you know how to get it… and hold on to it. Hear what I say?

**JUNE BAILEY:** *(Laughing)* Clever.

**KILLER:** As a man listens, he learns.

**JUNE BAILEY:** He mimics.

**KILLER:** Here we go dancin'.

**JUNE BAILEY:** Yep. I might say… if a man has Girlena, he might go dancing.

**KILLER:** You got that right, June Bailey.

**JUNE BAILEY:** If he can hold on to her.

**KILLER:** He can if he eliminates his obstacles.

*(LIGHTNING.*
*THUNDER.)*

**JUNE BAILEY:** *(Looking at the sky)* Storm's coming. I love the power of a storm. Nature forces a man to give respect. Nature has a way of humbling a man. Be something man could harness all that power.

**KILLER:** He can ... he can become the storm.

**JUNE BAILEY:** I'd like to see that. Hear what I say?

**KILLER:** *(Looking in window Right)* Baby if you live, your time will come.

**JUNE BAILEY:** Twelve years. That's a long time. I was working at J & L Steel when you... went away. I was working that graveyard shift. What you gonna do now?

**KILLER:** *(Crossing to window and looking in)* Find Girlena. Find out when she coming back.

**JUNE BAILEY:** What if she don't want to come back?

**KILLER:** I'll bring her back.

*(LIGHTNING. THUNDER.)*

**KILLER:** *(Pause)* You ever been locked up, June Bailey?

**JUNE BAILEY:** Can't say that I have. I always tried to avoid... bars.

**KILLER:** They did me a favor when they locked me up. I learned all about me, Charles Davis. I never would have found out things about me if I had stayed on East 55th. They locked me in a cell but all they did was free up my mind. I didn't have to worry about when it was time -- when it was time to eat, sleep or play. They did all that for me. For twelve years my mind was free. They took care of time. I just let time pass. They say time waits for no man, well time waited for me. While I was locked up I played numbers. I ran numbers. I cut numbers. 845. 724. 902. I changed numbers. 426 to 624, 721 to 127. I fired the Massario Brothers. Moved into their mansion. See, I lived dreams, created dreams, destroyed dreams. I drove a Fleetwood, lived in Hollywood. My name was Willie Haywood. I wrote the lyrics to the song, "Dr. Feelgood." I wore three piece silk suits, pork pie hats, and snakeskin shoes. I ate prime rib, lobster tail and crab legs. I caught a touchdown pass from Johnny Unitas. I sparred with Ali, dunked on Wilt, and hit a grand slam home run off Sandy Kofax in the seventh game of the World Series. I had a summer home next to the Kennedy's in Hyannis. I shot craps with President Johnson in Ellis Bar, and sat next to the nigger that killed Malcolm X. (Pause) Bought the gun that killed Fast Eddie Cain. I lived a thousand times over and over, and always came back... a hero...

**JUNE BAILEY:** You never thought about the reason why you were locked up?

**KILLER:** I knew why. A moment of anger. A moment's bad decision. In that moment, I became a raging storm.

*(LIGHTNING. THUNDER.)*

**JUNE BAILEY:** *(Looking at sky)* The power of the mind.

**KILLER:** Every time I close my eyes I see Girlena. The wind's blowing through her hair like a baby butterfly skipping through green grass. There's a scent of cherry in the air from her mother's perfume she's wearing. And, of course, she's standing on the prettiest pair of bow legs ever seen on man or beast. She's standing by the only good basketball hoop y'all used to play on. Never played on that hoop.

**JUNE BAILEY:** They only selected the best players. You know that, Killer. It was real competitive down there.

**KILLER:** Like in high school?

**JUNE BAILEY:** *(Pause)* Like in '55

**KILLER:** *(Pause)* Hear Girlena got a child now… a daughter.

**JUNE BAILEY:** Gabby.

**KILLER:** Gabriella. Eleven?

**JUNE:** Yep.

**KILLER:** Eleven. *(Pause)* Hear Fast Eddie Cain is her daddy?

**JUNE:** That's what Girlena say.

**KILLER:** *(Pulling gun and placing it to June Bailey's head)* What you say, nigger?

**JUNE BAILEY:** I only know what she told me, Killer.

**KILLER:** Where she at?

**JUNE BAILEY:** She didn't tell me where they were going.

**KILLER:** Girlena tell you everything, June Bailey.

**JUNE BAILEY:** She didn't tell me that.

**KILLER:** Ever had a gun to your head, June Bailey?

**JUNE BAILEY:** I've looked down the barrel of a gun before. Who living on East 55th hasn't?

**KILLER:** What happened?

**JUNE BAILEY:** Ricks had my back. Ricks always got my back.

**KILLER:** Not this time, June Bailey.

**JUNE BAILEY:** You never know, Killer. You never know.

**KILLER:** Ha. Ha. *(Putting gun away)* I'm gonna find Girlena. Bring her back. East 55th is where she belongs.

*(LIGHTNING.*
*THUNDER.)*

**JUNE BAILEY:** I figured you'd be here today or tomorrow.

**KILLER:** I been here three weeks, June Bailey.

**JUNE BAILEY:** Three weeks?

*(LIGHTNING. THUNDER.)*

**KILLER:** Been watchin' and waitin'. Thinkin' and plannin'. I learned to travel at night, June Bailey. Travel in the dark. Did you know bats can see real clear in the dark? I got eyes like the bat. *(Laughing)* Twenty-twenty. I saw you walking with your cane every night. Seen Old Johnny Dollar hopping along in those snakeskin shoes he wears, two sizes too small. Seen all the regulars filing out of Troy's. They all grinning cause they think Troy done solved their problems. Seen all them lames and squares picketing in front of Sealtest. Sealtest ain't never gonna hire no niggers, and niggers still gonna be drinking their sweet milk and eating their cottage cheese. I used to see Fast Eddie Cain rolling down East 43$^{rd}$ in that yellow GTO. *(Pause)* Don't see that no more. I seen him laying in that pretty yellow coffin though. Seen 'em carry out the body of that junkie teammate of yours after he OD'd on the roof with Big Edgar. And I seen Girlena walking on that fine pair of legs of hers. It's something to see the way she struts around on 'em *(Pause)* I seen Gabriella. Gonna be a heart breaker like her momma.

**JUNE BAILEY:** I hope you find her.

**KILLER:** The hell you do. But it don't matter, June Bailey. *(Pause)* I know she's in Chicago. I know she and Gabby took that double decker Greyhound to Chicago. Gabby carrying that basketball. Girlena carrying a brown bag of fried chicken. Girlena could always fry up some chicken. I got a taste for some right now.

**JUNE BAILEY:** Gabby's my daughter, Killer.

*(LIGHTNING. THUNDER.)*

**KILLER:** What?

**JUNE BAILEY:** She's my daughter.

**KILLER:** Eddie Cain was Gabriella's father. That's why he's dead.

**JUNE BAILEY:** I ain't lyin.

**KILLER:** Well you just damn better be.

**JUNE BAILEY:** Girlena and I always been... close... like brother and sister. You know that... Everybody around here knows that, but... she did affect me though... the way a woman affects a man. Girlena and I almost hooked up in '55. While we were celebrating that State Championship. Troy took the whole team and the cheerleaders to some fancy fish fry after that game. We didn't leave Columbus 'til late... left in the middle of a snowstorm. Took us eight hours to get back to Cleveland, but who cared. We were the '55 State Champs. It was pitch black 'cept for the layers of falling snow. We watched the snowflakes dance across the headlights of our charter bus, as it was making its way down highway 71. Everyone else on the bus was asleep. Girlena was sitting next to me. We snuggled to keep warm. We kissed... once... and then we kissed again... and again... God, the feeling was incredible... I started to rub the raised letters of East Tech on her cheerleader sweater... and beneath it... her breasts... she moaned... Her skirt was up slightly, revealing her pretty brown thighs and legs... then the damn bus pulled into the school parking lot, followed by a long procession of parents, fans, well-wishers... Troy's old pick up honking in honor of the '55 State Champs. The interior lights of the bus came on. It didn't happen that night. *(Pause)* But three years later, a summer storm hit East 55th in early June, the worst summer storm anyone around here -- anyone can remember... rain... lightning... thunder... and the wind... Troy's corner store was somehow the only place on the entire block with electricity... The electric company restored power to all the white neighborhoods first... so we went without power for seven days and seven nights... seven nights with flashlights and candlelight and no fans... no fans in over hundred degree temperatures... no fans 'cause we had no electricity. You remember that first night? Girlena called you and begged you to come to her, begged you to stay with her... She was really afraid that night... that first night of the worst summer storm anyone around here can remember. You promised you'd come, stay with her... but you never showed up. I stayed with Girlena... that first night... the only night... it happened... Eleven years ago Gabby was born. She's my daughter.

*(LIGHTNING. THUNDER.)*

**JUNE BAILEY:** *(Turning away, crossing, and looking up)* Looks like another summer storm.

**KILLER:** *(Taking out gun, pointing it at him, and pulling back trigger)* Here we go dancin'.

*(A loud clap of thunder and single gunshot are heard as security light goes out momentarily and the backyard area becomes dark. After a few moments the light comes back*

*on revealing Killer Davis on ground, mortally wounded. Ricks enters.)*

**JUNE BAILEY:** Thought you were in Chicago with Girlena and Gabby?

**RICKS:** *(Putting his gun away)* I got on board the Greyhound with them and sat 'til it was time for the bus to pull out. Girlena and I decided I better get back to East 55th Street and cover your sorry ass like I've been doing since we were in elementary school. I'll go up there later. What we gonna do now?

**JUNE BAILEY:** *(Sitting)* I'll call Troy. He'll know what to do. *(Pause)* Ricks, I been doing a lot thinking about '55. Been doing a lot of thinking about them Massario Brothers up there in Little Italy, too. *(Pause)* I'm goin' back up that hill.

**RICKS:** I know. *(To him)* Let me know when we going back up there...

*(June Bailey picks up a basketball and nods. Ricks rests his hand on June Bailey's shoulder as they look towards the basketball hoop. June Bailey places his hand over Ricks' hand.)*

**JUNE BAILEY:** Here we go... Dancin'.

*(Lights fade to black.)*

**THE END**

*More Great Plays From
Original Works Publishing*

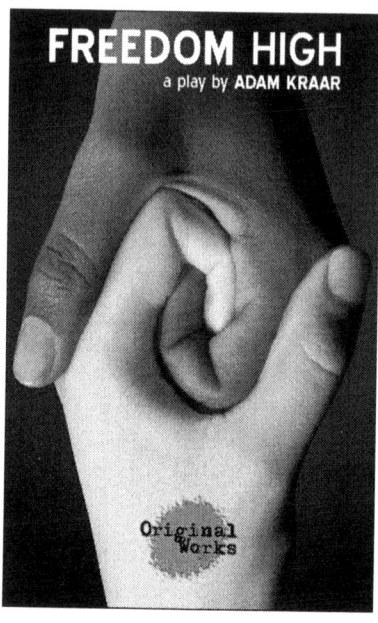

## Freedom High
### By Adam Kraar

**Synopsis:** Inspired by actual events, FREEDOM HIGH takes place in June 1964, when black Civil Rights workers trained hundreds of white volunteers to work in Mississippi registering blacks to vote. Jessica, a young white volunteer, has no idea has no idea how dangerous – both physically and emotionally – the project will be. Instead, she throws herself into learning non-violent tactics and stubbornly trying to befriend an angry, wounded veteran of the Movement.

When three Civil Rights workers who'd been at the training the previous week disappear, the volunteers are forced to decide if they can risk their lives for a mission that seems doomed. Jessica discovers the deep – sometimes dark – complexity of her motivations, and those of everyone else involved.

**Cast Size:** 4 Males, 3 Females (with doubling). Up to 16 actors may be used

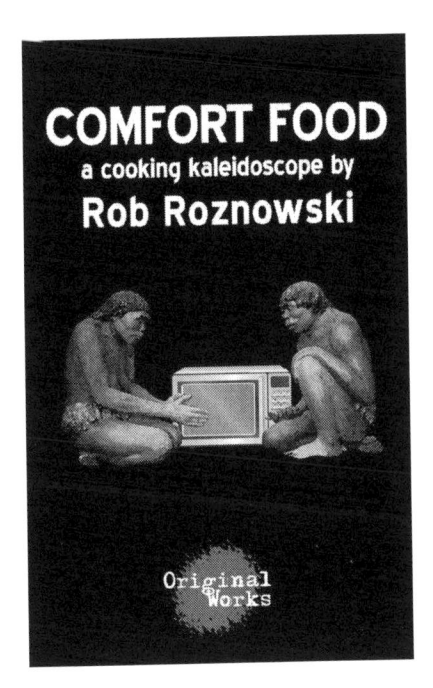

## Comfort Food by Rob Roznowski

**Synopsis:** Comfort Food is a comedy that explores the intersection of food and history. A collection of scenes told in reverse chronological order, decade by decade, back to the first published American cookbook. Funny and insightful vignettes include the rise of the microwave in relation to women's lib, the swinging 60s mixing with fondue parties, and bread lines contrasting with cocktail parties in the 1930s.

**Cast Size:** Diverse cast of 6 - 20

**Militant Language** by Sean Christopher Lewis

**Synopsis:** Set in modern Iraq, this savage contemporary fable ignites when a pair of American soldiers return from a routine surveillance detail covered in blood. The barracks are no safe haven. The Captain fights to control his troops as they walk the high-wires of a secret homosexual affair, the sexual abuse of a female soldier, a missing Iraqi boy, and a baby found in the desert, ala Moses. This play explores how violence begets violence, lies beget lies, truth is born from trust, and understanding war makes as much sense as sand raining from the heavens.

**Cast Size:** 5 Males, 1 Female

# NOTES

# NOTES

# NOTES

Made in the USA
Middletown, DE
19 July 2016